Nick Vandome

iPhone
for Seniors

6th edition

covers all iPhones with iOS 13

In easy steps is an imprint of In Easy Steps Limited
16 Hamilton Terrace · Holly Walk · Leamington Spa
Warwickshire · United Kingdom · CV32 4LY
www.ineasysteps.com

Sixth Edition

Notice of Liability
Every effort has been made to ensure that this book contains accurate
and current information. However, In Easy Steps Limited and the
author shall not be liable for any loss or damage suffered by readers
as a result of any information contained herein.

Trademarks
iPhone® is a registered trademark of Apple Computer, Inc. All other
trademarks are acknowledged as belonging to their respective
companies.

In Easy Steps Limited supports The Forest Stewardship Council (FSC),
the leading international forest certification organization. All our titles
that are printed on Greenpeace approved FSC certified paper carry the
FSC logo.

MIX
Paper from
responsible sources
FSC® C020837

Printed and bound in the United Kingdom

ISBN 978-1-84078-862-4

Contents

1 Your New iPhone

The iPhone is a sleek, stylish smartphone that is ideal for anyone, of any age. This chapter introduces the three models of the iPhone, and takes you through its buttons and controls. It also shows how to set it up, ready for use.

Hands on with the iPhone

The iPhone is one of the great success stories of the digital age. It is one of the world's leading smartphones: a touchscreen phone that can be used for not only making calls and sending text messages, but also for online access and a huge range of tasks through the use of apps. Essentially, the iPhone is a powerful, compact computer that can be used for everything you need in your mobile life.

The latest range of iPhones includes the iPhone 11, and the iPhone 11 Pro and 11 Pro Max. All models use the iOS 13 operating system, and the A13 Bionic chip processor.

iPhone 11

This is an upgrade to the previous standard range of iPhone. Its specifications include:

- **Screen**: The iPhone 11 has a **6.1 inch** (measured diagonally) Liquid Retina HD display screen.

- **Storage**: This determines how much content you can store on your iPhone. For the iPhone 11, the storage capacity options are: 64GB, 128GB or 256GB.

- **Camera**. A dual lens 12-megapixel (MP) camera for taking photos, and a front-facing 12MP TrueDepth camera for selfies, videos and for use with Face ID.

- **Face ID**. Unlock the iPhone by looking at the screen.

- **Battery power**: The iPhone 11 provides up to 65 hours of wireless audio playback, 17 hours' video playback, 10 hours' video streaming, and fast charging capability.

- **Input/Output**: There is a Lightning Connector port (for charging, headphones, and connecting to a computer); a built-in speaker; and a built-in microphone.

- **Water resistant.** Water resistant up to 2 meters for up to 30 minutes. Also splash- and dust-resistant.

- **Sensors**: The sensors are: accelerometer, barometer, ambient light sensor, proximity sensor, and gyroscope.

This latest range of iPhones has no Home button. The functions that were previously undertaken by the Home button are done by a range of gestures on the screen, and by using the buttons on the body of the iPhone. See pages 16-18 for details about these gestures. For older iPhones that have a physical Home button and run iOS 13, the relevant commands will also be listed throughout the book.

The New icon pictured above indicates a new or enhanced feature introduced with the iPhone 11, 11 Pro, 11 Pro Max or the latest version of its operating system, iOS 13.

iPhone 11 Pro

This is the first iPhone with Pro in its designation. Its specifications include:

- **Screen**: The iPhone 11 Pro has a **5.8 inch** (measured diagonally) Super Retina XDR display screen.

- **Storage**: This determines how much content you can store on your iPhone. For the iPhone 11 Pro, the storage capacity options are: 64GB, 256GB or 512GB.

- **Camera**. A triple lens 12MP camera for taking photos, and a front-facing 12MP TrueDepth camera for taking selfies, videos and for use with Face ID.

- **Face ID**. Unlock the iPhone by looking at the screen.

- **Battery power**: The iPhone 11 Pro provides up to 65 hours of wireless audio playback, 18 hours' video playback, 11 hours' video streaming, and fast charging capability.

- **Input/Output**: These are a Lightning Connector port (for charging, headphones and connecting to a computer), built-in speaker and a built-in microphone.

- **Water resistant.** Water resistant up to 4 meters for up to 30 minutes. Also splash- and dust-resistant.

- **Sensors**: The sensors are: accelerometer, barometer, ambient light sensor, proximity sensor, and gyroscope.

The amount of storage you need may change once you have bought your iPhone. If possible, buy a version with as much storage as your budget allows.

Face ID for unlocking the iPhone is available on the full range of the latest iPhone models; i.e. iPhone 11, 11 Pro and 11 Pro Max. For details about setting this up, see page 24.

None of the latest range of iPhones has a separate headphone jack: this is accommodated using the Lightning Connector port.

...cont'd

All iPhone models have connectivity for fast 802.11ax Wi-Fi, 4G/3G, and Bluetooth 5.0.

All three of the latest iPhones can be connected to a High Definition (HD) TV with AirPlay Mirroring and an Apple TV box. This then displays whatever is on your iPhone on the TV screen.

To connect your iPhone to an HDTV you will need an Apple Lightning/ Digital AV adapter, an Apple Lightning/ VGA adapter, or an Apple Lightning/HDMI adapter (sold separately).

iPhone 11 Pro Max

This is a larger version of the iPhone 11 Pro, and has the same camera system and the longest battery life of any iPhone to date. Its specifications include:

- **Screen**: The iPhone 11 Pro Max has a **6.5 inch** (measured diagonally) Super Retina XDR display screen.

- **Storage**: This determines how much content you can store on your iPhone. The iPhone 11 Pro Max the storage capacity options are: 64GB, 256GB or 512GB.

- **Camera**. A triple lens 12MP camera for taking photos, and a front-facing 12MP TrueDepth camera for taking selfies, videos and for use with Face ID.

- **Face ID**. Unlock the iPhone by looking at the screen.

- **Battery power**: The iPhone 11 Pro Max provides up to 80 hours of wireless audio playback, 20 hours' video playback, 12 hours' video streaming, and fast charging capability.

- **Input/Output**: These are a Lightning Connector port (for charging, headphones and connecting to a computer), built-in speaker and a built-in microphone.

- **Water resistant.** Water resistant up to 4 meters for up to 30 minutes. Also splash- and dust-resistant.

- **Sensors**: The sensors are: accelerometer, barometer, ambient light sensor, proximity sensor, and gyroscope.

What do you get?

The iPhone box contains all of the items required to use your new iPhone, charge it, and open the SIM tray to add a SIM card. The various components are:

- **iPhone**. The iPhone will be turned off, but there should be enough charge in the battery to turn it on without having to charge it first.

- **The Lightning to USB-C cable**. This can be used for charging the iPhone, or connecting it to a computer for downloading items.

- **The EarPods**. These can be used to listen to audio items on your iPhone. They can also be used to manage phone calls using the central control button (see page 56 for details). There is no headphone jack for the latest iPhone EarPods, as they connect via the Lightning Connector.

- **The SIM tool**. This is a small metal gadget that is in a cardboard envelope in the iPhone box. It is used to open the SIM tray so that a SIM card can be inserted (see pages 14-15 for details).

There is a wide range of accessories for the iPhone. These include cases in a range of colors and materials. These cases give some protection to the body of your iPhone.

To charge your iPhone with the Lightning to USB cable: insert the Lightning Connector into the bottom of the iPhone, and insert the USB-C connector into the plug that is also provided in the iPhone box. Connect the plug to a socket to charge your iPhone.

The latest iPhones support wireless charging, by placing the device on a compatible base station.

iPhone Nuts and Bolts

On/Off (Side) button

The button for turning the iPhone On and Off (and putting it into Sleep mode) is located on the top right-hand side of the body (looking at the screen). As with other buttons on the body, it is slightly raised to make it easier to locate just by touch.

Don't forget

For more details on turning on the iPhone, see page 16.

Volume controls

Volume is controlled using two separate buttons on the left-hand side of the body. They do not have symbols on them but they are used to increase and decrease the volume.

Ringer/silent (use this to turn the ringer On or Off for when a call or a notification is received)

Volume up

Volume down

Don't forget

To make phone calls with your iPhone you need to have an active SIM card inserted, and a suitable service provider for cellular (mobile) calls and data. The iPhone 11, 11 Max and 11 Max Pro use a nano SIM card, which is smaller than both the standard size and the micro size.

Top notch

All iPhones have a notch at the top of the screen that accommodates the TrueDepth camera, sensors for use with Face ID, built-in stereo speakers, and a built-in microphone.

Lightning Connector, speakers and microphone

These are located at the bottom of the iPhone.

Stereo speakers

Microphone   Lightning Connector

Back view of the iPhone

This contains the main camera, the LED flash, and the rear microphone.

iPhone 11

Main camera. This is a dual lens camera.

Rear microphone

LED flash (and torch)

iPhone 11 Pro and 11 Pro Max

The camera on the iPhone 11 Pro and 11 Pro Max has three lenses for the main camera: one ultra wide-angle, one wide angle and one telephoto. They combine to take each shot. This produces the highest quality photos yet on an iPhone, with a range of options, such Ultra Wide. See page 104 for more details.

Don't forget

The main camera on all iPhone 11 models is a high-quality 12-megapixel camera. It can capture excellent photos and also 4K (ultra-high definition) and high definition (HD) video. The front-facing TrueDepth camera has a 12-megapixel resolution and can be used for taking "selfies"; the modern craze of taking a photo of yourself and then posting it online on a social media site such as Facebook. It is also used for the Face ID functionality for unlocking the iPhone (see page 24), and for FaceTime video calls (see pages 126-127).

13

Inserting the SIM

The phone services for the iPhone are provided by companies that enable access to their mobile networks, which you will be able to use for phone calls, texts, and mobile data for access to the internet. Companies provide different packages: you can buy the iPhone for a reduced sum and then pay a monthly contract; typically for 12 or 24 months. Despite the fact that the initial outlay for the iPhone will be cheaper, this works out more expensive over the period of the contract. Another option is to buy the iPhone (make sure it is unlocked so that you can use any SIM card) and use a SIM-only offer. This way, you can buy a package that suits you for calls, texts and mobile data. Look for offers that have unlimited data for internet access.

The SIM card for the iPhone will be provided by your mobile carrier; i.e. the company that provides your cellular phone and data services. Without this, you would still be able to communicate with your iPhone, but only via Wi-Fi and compatible services. A SIM card gives you access to a mobile network too. Some iPhones come with the SIM pre-installed, but you can also insert one yourself. To do this:

1 Take the SIM tool out of the iPhone box and remove it from its cardboard packaging

2 Insert the SIM tool into the small hole on the SIM slot on the side of the iPhone

3 Press the tool firmly into the hole so that the SIM tray pops out and starts to appear. Pull the SIM tray fully out

4 Place the SIM card with the metal contacts face downwards (shown facing upwards in the image). Place the SIM tray in position so that the diagonal cut is in the same position as the cut on the SIM card

Hot tip

If you lose the SIM tool you can use the end of a stretched-out paper clip instead.

5 Place the SIM card into the SIM tray. It should fit flush, resting on a narrow ridge underneath it, with the diagonal cut on the card matching the cut in the tray

Beware

The SIM tray can only be inserted in one way. If it appears to encounter resistance, do not force it; take it out and try again. The hole in the SIM tray should be nearest to the bottom of the phone body.

6 Place your thumb over the bottom of the SIM tray, covering the SIM card, and place the tray into the SIM slot, with the metal contacts facing the back of the phone. Push the tray firmly into the slot until it clicks into place

Don't forget

For older iPhones that have a physical Home button and run iOS 13, some of the functionality on these three pages is achieved with the Home button. These instances will be noted throughout the book.

Hot tip

If your iPhone ever freezes, or if something is not working properly, it can be rebooted by pressing the Volume Up button, then the Volume Down button, then pressing and holding the On/Off button.

Beware

The color of the bar at the bottom of the screen, for returning to the Home screen, is dependent on the background color of the app being used. If it has a light background, the bar will be a dark color; if it has a dark background the bar will be a light color.

iPhone Gestures

None of the iPhone 11 models have a Home button and, as with the previous range of iPhones, the actions that were previously accessed by pressing the Home button are performed by gestures on the screen and actions using the On/Off and Volume buttons. Gestures for the iPhone include the following (also including some general iPhone actions):

Turning on

Press and hold on the On/Off button for a few seconds. Keep it pressed until the Apple icon appears. This will display the Lock screen (see page 23 for more on using the Lock Screen).

Unlocking the iPhone

This is done by using Face ID. Once this has been set up (see pages 24-25), raise the phone so that the camera can view your face, and simultaneously swipe up from the bottom of the screen, to view the last viewed screen.

Returning to the Home screen

Swipe up from the bar at the bottom of the screen. This can be done from any app.

Accessing the Control Center

To access the Control Center of useful widgets, swipe down from the top right-hand corner of the screen. (On older models of iPhone, this was achieved by swiping up from the bottom of the screen, which now returns you to the Home screen.)

Buy a glass screen protector to help preserve your iPhone's screen. This will help prevent marks and scratches, and can also save the screen if it is broken: the protector breaks rather than the iPhone's screen itself.

Accessing the Notification Center

The Notification Center is accessed by swiping down from the top left-hand corner or the middle of the screen.

Accessing Siri

Press and hold the On/Off button until Siri appears. Alternatively, use the Hey Siri function (see pages 40-41).

Accessing the App Switcher

Swipe up from the bottom of the screen and pause in the middle of the screen to view open and recently-used apps.

17

...cont'd

Reachability

To use Reachability, which moves the items on the screen to the bottom half, to make them easier to access with one hand, swipe down from the bottom of the screen (see page 44 for more details).

Hot tip

Screenshots are saved to the **Photos** app. They can be viewed here from the **Photos** button on the bottom toolbar and also the **Screenshots** album in the **Albums** section.

Taking a screenshot

To capture an image of what is currently on the screen, quickly press and release the On/Off button and the Volume Up button simultaneously. For older iPhones that have a physical Home button and run iOS 13, a screenshot can be captured by pressing the On/Off button and the Home button simultaneously.

Paying with Apple Pay

To use Apple Pay to pay for items with your iPhone, double-click the On/Off button, and authorize with Face ID. See pages 54-55 for details about setting up Apple Pay.

Don't forget

For older iPhones that have a physical Home button and run iOS 13, press and hold the On/Off button and access the **slide to power off** button.

Turning off

Press and hold the On/Off button and either of the volume buttons until the Power Off screen appears. Swipe the **slide to power off** button to the right to turn off the iPhone.

Getting Set Up

When you first turn on your iPhone there will be a series of setup screens. These include the following options:

- **Language**. Select the language you want to use.

- **Country**. Select the country in which you are located.

- **Quick Start**. This can be used to transfer settings from another compatible iOS device.

- **Wi-Fi network**. Connect to the internet, using either your own home network or a public Wi-Fi hotspot.

- **Data & Privacy**. This is used to identify features that ask for your personal information.

- **Face ID.** Use this to create a Face ID for unlocking your iPhone by looking at it while swiping up from the bottom of the screen. See page 24 for details.

- **Create Passcode**. This can be used to create a numerical passcode for unlocking your iPhone.

- **Apps & Data**. This can be used to set up an iPhone from an iCloud backup, or as a new iPhone.

- **Apple ID and iCloud**. This can be used to use an existing iCloud account or to create a new one.

- **Keep your iPhone Up to Date**. This can be used to install updates to the operating system (iOS) automatically.

- **Location Services**. This determines whether your iPhone can use your geographical location for apps.

- **Siri.** This can be used to set up Siri, the digital voice assistant, ready for use.

- **Screen Time**. This can be used to set limits for using apps on the iPhone and for creating a usage report.

- **iPhone and App Analytics**. This allows details from the iPhone and its apps to be sent to Apple and developers.

Most of the options available during the setup process can also be accessed within the **Settings** app.

For more information about using iCloud, see Chapter 3.

Beware

The Cellular (Mobile) Data settings contain the **Data Roaming** option (**Settings** > **Cellular** > **Cellular Data Options**): if you are traveling abroad you may want to turn this **Off** to avoid undue charges for when you are connected to the internet. If in doubt, contact your provider before you go.

Hot tip

Your iPhone's display name is located at **Settings** > **General** > **About**, and can be changed here if required.

Hot tip

To change the iPhone's wallpaper, tap once on the **Choose a New Wallpaper** option in the **Wallpaper** setting.

iPhone Settings

The Settings app controls settings for the way the iPhone and its apps operate:

- **Apple ID, iCloud, iTunes & App Store**. Contains settings for these items.

- **Airplane Mode**. This can be used to disable network connectivity while on an airplane.

- **Wi-Fi**. This enables you to select a wireless network.

- **Bluetooth**. Turn this On to connect Bluetooth devices.

- **Cellular (Mobile) Data**. These are the settings that will be used with your cellular (mobile) service provider.

- **Personal Hotspot**. This can be used to share your internet connection.

- **Notifications**. This determines how the Notification Center operates (see pages 26-27).

- **Sounds & Haptics**. This has options for setting sounds for alerts and actions such as tapping on the keyboard.

- **Do Not Disturb**. Use this to specify times when you do not want to receive audio alerts, phone calls, and video calls.

- **Screen Time**. Options for reporting on and limiting iPhone usage.

- **General**. This contains a range of common settings.

- **Control Center**. This determines how the Control Center operates (see pages 34-37).

- **Display & Brightness**. This can be used to set the screen brightness, text size, and bold text.

- **Accessibility**. his can be used for users with visual or motor issues.

- **Wallpaper**. This can be used to select a wallpaper.

- **Siri & Search**. Options for the digital voice assistant.

- **Face ID & Passcode**. This has options for adding a passcode or fingerprint ID for unlocking the iPhone.

- **Emergency SOS.** This can be used to set an Auto Call to an emergency number.

- **Battery**. This can be used to view battery usage by apps.

- **Privacy**. This can be used to activate Location Services so that your location can be used by specific apps.

- **iTunes & App Store**. This can be used to specify downloading options for the iTunes and App Stores.

- **Wallet & Apple Pay**. This can be used to add credit or debit cards for use with Apple Pay (see pages 54-55).

- **Passwords & Accounts.** This contains options for managing website passwords and adding online accounts.

- **Mail**, **Contacts**, **Calendars**. These are three separate settings that have options for how these apps operate.

iPhone app settings

Most of the built-in iPhone apps have their own settings that determine how the apps operate. These include: Notes, Reminders, Voice Memos, Phone, Messages, FaceTime, Maps, Compass, Measure, Safari, News, Stocks, Health, Shortcuts, Music,

Settings	
Notes	>
Reminders	>
Voice Memos	>
Phone	>
Messages	>
FaceTime	>
Maps	>

TV, Photos, Camera, Books and Podcasts. Tap on one of these tabs to view the settings for that app. (Apps that are downloaded from the App Store also have their individual settings in this location in the Settings app.)

If a Settings option has an On/Off button next to it, this can be changed by swiping the button to either the left or right. Green indicates that the option is **On**. Select **Settings > Accessibility > Display & Text Size > On/Off Labels** to show or hide icons on each button.

Tap on a link to see additional options:

DISPLAY ZOOM	
View	Standard

Tap once here to move back to the previous page for the selected setting:

‹ Settings	**Display & Brightness**
BRIGHTNESS	

21

About iOS 13

iOS 13 is the latest operating system for the iPhone.

You will need an Apple ID for all Apple online services. This is free – to register go to **https://appleid.apple. com**

Tap on **Create Your Apple ID**. You will be prompted to enter your email address and a password. Then follow the on-screen instructions. Tap on **Create Apple ID** when ready.

To check the version of the iOS, look in **Settings** > **General** > **Software Update**.

iOS 13 is the latest version of the operating system for Apple's mobile devices including all of the latest iPhone 11 models.

iOS 13 further enhances the user experience for which the mobile operating system is renowned. This includes:

- **Dark Mode**. This can be used to invert the color of the iPhone's screen, so that the items on it can be easier to read, particularly in the evening.

- **Camera and Photos.** The range of iPhone 11 models offer sophisticated camera options for taking high quality photos. In conjunction with this, the Photos app has powerful new editing tools so that a greater range of editing techniques can be applied to photos. Many of the same editing effects can also be applied to videos.

- **Updated apps**. Several apps have been given an overhaul in iOS 13, including: the Reminders app, which has a new interface for viewing all of the reminders and lists that have been created; the Health app, which has been redesigned so that it is easier to access new content; the Safari app, which has been redesigned so that there are now more options when viewing web pages; the Photos app, which has a new design for viewing photos, videos and collated collections; and the Maps app, which can now be used to set a greater range of favorite locations.

- **Improved messaging**. The Messages app can now be used to create a greater range of animated icons of yourself (memojis) and the keyboard can be used for QuickPath typing, where letters can be selected simply by swiping over them.

- **Performance and Privacy**. iOS 13 contains a range of unseen performance enhancements, making it faster for unlocking your iPhone and also launching apps. Also, the privacy features have been enhanced, to allow you to give apps access to your location just once.

Using the Lock Screen

To save power, it is possible to set your iPhone screen to auto-lock. This is the equivalent of the Sleep option on a traditional computer. To do this:

1 Tap once on the **Settings** app

2 Tap once on the **Display & Brightness** tab

AA Display & Brightness

3 Tap once on the **Auto-Lock** option

Auto-Lock	Never >

4 Tap once on the time of non-use after which you wish the screen to be locked

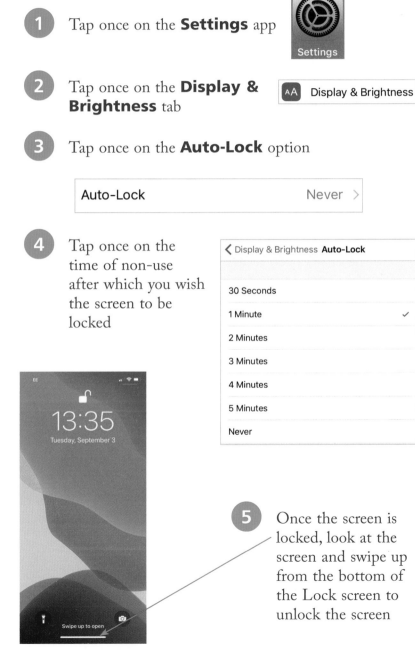

‹ Display & Brightness **Auto-Lock**

30 Seconds

1 Minute ✓

2 Minutes

3 Minutes

4 Minutes

5 Minutes

Never

5 Once the screen is locked, look at the screen and swipe up from the bottom of the Lock screen to unlock the screen

The screen can also be locked by pressing once on the **On/Off** button on the right-hand side of the iPhone's body.

For older iPhones that have a physical Home button and run iOS 13, the iPhone is unlocked by pressing the Home button once if Touch ID has been set up (**Settings** > **Touch ID and Passcode**).

Swipe from right to left on the Lock screen to access the camera.

Face ID and Passcode

With the removal of the Home button on the latest range of iPhones, the means of unlocking the phone is done through the use of Face ID. If this cannot be used for any reason, a passcode can be entered instead. To set up Face ID:

Hot tip

Face ID can also be used for contactless purchases for Apple Pay (see pages 54-55), and purchases in the iTunes and App Store. Drag the buttons **On** as required under the **Use Face ID For** heading in the **Face ID & Passcode** settings.

USE FACE ID FOR:	
iPhone Unlock	⬤
iTunes & App Store	⬤
Apple Pay	⬤
Password AutoFill	⬤

Don't forget

For older iPhones that have a physical Home button and run iOS 13, the Touch ID feature is used, rather than Face ID (**Settings > Touch ID and Passcode**).

1 Select **Settings** > **Face ID & Passcode**

☺ Face ID & Passcode

2 Tap once on the **Set Up Face ID** button

Set Up Face ID

3 Position your face in the center of the circle that accesses the iPhone's camera. Move your head slowly in a circle so that the camera can record all elements of your face

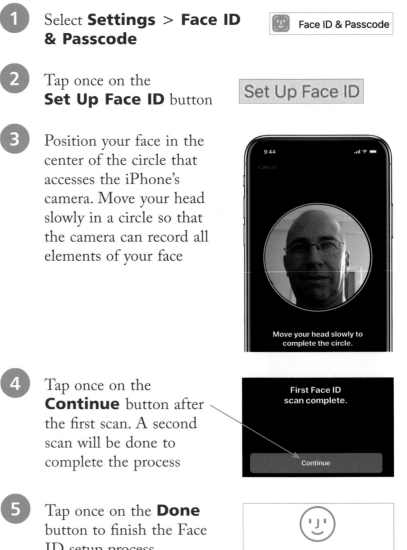

Move your head slowly to complete the circle.

4 Tap once on the **Continue** button after the first scan. A second scan will be done to complete the process

First Face ID scan complete.

Continue

5 Tap once on the **Done** button to finish the Face ID setup process

Face ID is now set up.

Done

Adding a passcode

If Face ID cannot be used to unlock the iPhone, a numerical passcode can be used instead. This has to be set up at the same time as creating a Face ID. To do this:

1 Select **Settings** > **Face ID & Passcode**

| Face ID & Passcode |

2 Tap once on the **Turn Passcode On** button

‹ Settings	**Passcode Lock**
Turn Passcode On	
Change Passcode	
Require Passcode	Immediately ›

3 Enter a six-digit passcode. This can be used to unlock your iPhone from the Lock screen

Set Passcode	Cancel

Enter a passcode

● ● ● ● ○ ○

Passcode Options

1	2 ABC	3 DEF
4 GHI	5 JKL	6 MNO
7 PQRS	8 TUV	9 WXYZ
	0	⌫

4 Once a passcode

Require Passcode	Immediately ›

has been created, tap once on the **Require Passcode** button in Step 2 to specify a time period until the passcode is required on the Lock screen. The best option is **Immediately**, otherwise someone else could access your iPhone

Beware

If you use a passcode to lock your iPhone write it down, but store it in a location away from the iPhone.

Don't forget

Tap once on the **Passcode Options** link in Step 3 to access other options for creating a passcode. These include a **Custom Alphanumeric Code**, a **Custom Numeric Code**, and a **4-Digit Code**. The 4-Digit Code is the least secure, and the Alphanumeric Code is the most secure, as it can use a combination of numbers, letters and symbols.

Notifications

Notifications can be used with iOS 13 so that you never miss an important message or update. Notifications can be viewed in the Notification Center and also on the Lock screen. To set up and use Notifications:

Hot tip

The Notification Center can be accessed by dragging down from the top left-hand corner or the middle of the screen, in any app.

Hot tip

Turn the **Lock Screen** option to **On** in Step 4 to enable notifications for the selected app to be displayed even when the iPhone is locked.

Hot tip

Text messages can be replied to directly from the Lock screen, without unlocking the iPhone. To do this, press on the message on the Lock screen and compose a reply as normal.

1 Tap once on the **Settings** app

2 Tap once on the **Notifications** tab

3 Under **Notification Style**, tap once on an item to select the notification settings for a specific app

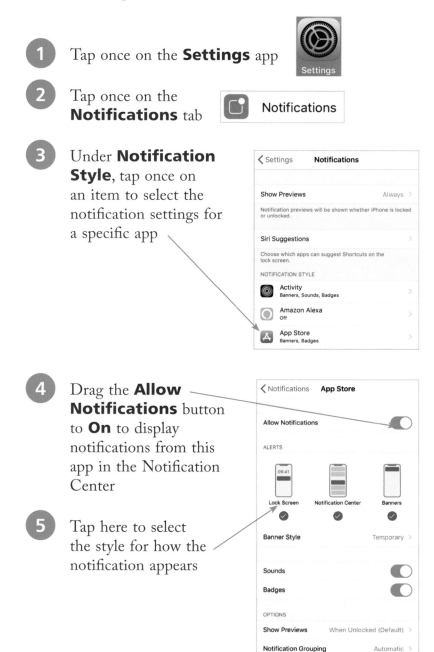

4 Drag the **Allow Notifications** button to **On** to display notifications from this app in the Notification Center

5 Tap here to select the style for how the notification appears

6 Swipe down from the top left or middle of the iPhone screen, from the Home screen or any app, to view your notifications in the Notification Center. This is split into two sections: the notifications page, which contains notifications from the apps in Step 3 opposite; and the Today View page that contains widgets with real-time information about topics such as the weather, stocks, and news; the Up Next calendar item; and notifications from the apps. Swipe right and left to move between the two pages

The Today View screen in Step 6 (second image) can be viewed from the Home screen by swiping from left to right.

 7 Swipe to the bottom of the widgets page, and tap once on the **Edit** button to manage the widgets that appear here. Tap on a red circle to delete a widget from the Today page, or scroll down and tap on a green button to add a new widget

At the bottom of the window in Step 5 on the previous page there is a **Notification Grouping** option. Set this to **Automatic**, so that all similar notifications are grouped together.

OPTIONS	
Show Previews	When Unlocked (Default) >
Notification Grouping	Automatic >

27

Updating Software

The operating system that powers the iPhone is known as iOS. This is a mobile computing operating system, and it is also used on the iPod Touch. The latest version is iOS 13. Periodically there are updates to the iOS to fix bugs and add new features. These can be downloaded to your iPhone once they are released:

Hot tip

It is always worth updating the iOS to keep up-to-date with fixes. Also, app developers update their products to use the latest iOS features.

1 Tap once on the **Settings** app

Settings

2 Tap once on the **General** tab
(a red tag indicates that an update is available)

⚙ General   1 ›

3 Tap once on the **Software Update** option

Software Update   1 ›

Hot tip

Software Update can be set to be performed automatically overnight, when the iPhone is charging and connected to Wi-Fi. Tap on the **Automatic Updates** button in Step 4 and drag the **Automatic Updates** button to On.

Automatic Updates

4 If there is an update available it will be displayed here, with details of what is contained within it

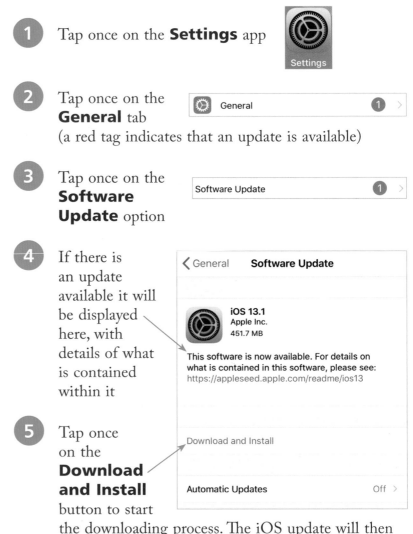

‹ General   **Software Update**

iOS 13.1
Apple Inc.
451.7 MB

This software is now available. For details on what is contained in this software, please see:
https://appleseed.apple.com/readme/ios13

Download and Install

Automatic Updates   Off ›

5 Tap once on the **Download and Install** button to start the downloading process. The iOS update will then be done automatically

2 Starting to use your iPhone

This chapter covers the functions on the iPhone that you need to use it confidently and make the most of its features. From opening and closing apps, using Screen Time to monitor your iPhone usage, and using Apple Pay, it explains the iPhone environment so you can quickly get up and running with it.

Opening and Closing Items

All apps on your iPhone can be opened with the minimum of fuss and effort:

The Home screen is the one that you see when you turn on your iPhone. There can be several additional Home screens, depending on the number of apps on the iPhone.

When you switch from one app to another, the first one stays open in the background. You can go back to it by accessing it from the App Switcher window or the Home screen.

For older iPhones that have a physical Home button and run iOS 13, press the Home button to return to the Home screen. To access the App Switcher, double-click the Home button.

1 Tap once on an icon to open the app

App Store

2 The app opens at its Home screen

Today

HOW TO
Make your life more efficient

3 Swipe up from the bottom of the screen to return to the iPhone Home screen. Swipe up from the bottom of the screen and pause in the middle of the screen to access the App Switcher

4 From the App Switcher window, swipe left and right between open apps, and tap on one to make it the active app. Swipe an app to the top of the window in the App Switcher to close it

Navigating Around

The iPhone screen is very receptive to touch, and this is the main method of navigating around, through a combination of swiping, tapping, and pinching.

Swiping between Home screens

Once you have added more apps to your iPhone, they will start to fill up more Home screens. To move between these, swipe left or right with one or two fingers to move between Home screens.

Swiping up and down

Swipe up and down with one finger to move up or down web pages, photos, maps or documents. The content moves in the opposite direction of the swipe; i.e. if you swipe up, the page will move down, and vice versa.

Pinching and swiping

Swipe outwards with thumb and forefinger to zoom in on a web page, photo, map or document. This enables you to zoom in on an item to a greater degree than double-tapping with one finger (see bottom tip).

Pinch together with thumb and forefinger to zoom back out on a web page, photo, map or document.

You can also move between different Home screens by tapping once on the small white dots in the middle of the screen above the Dock (see page 32).

The faster you swipe on the screen, the faster the screen moves up or down.

Double-tap with one finger to zoom in on a web page, photo, map or document. Double-tap with one finger to return to the original view.

Using the Dock

By default, there are four apps on the Dock at the bottom of the iPhone's screen. These are the four that Apple thinks you will use most frequently:

- **Phone**, for making and receiving calls.
- **Safari**, for web browsing.
- **Messages**, for text messaging.
- **Music**.

Hot tip

With iOS 13, some of the pre-installed (built-in) apps can be deleted from your iPhone. These are indicated by a cross in the top left-hand corner when you press and hold on an app.

You can rearrange the order in which the Dock apps appear:

 Press and hold on one of the Dock apps until it starts to jiggle

Hot tip

Just above the Dock is a line of small white dots. These indicate how many screens of content there are on the iPhone. Tap on one of the dots to go to that screen.

 Drag the app into its new position

 Swipe up from the bottom of the screen to exit editing mode

Adding and removing Dock apps

You can also remove apps from the Dock and add new ones:

 To remove an app from the Dock, press and hold it, and drag it onto the main screen area

If items are removed from the Dock they are still available in the same way from the main screen.

 To add an app to the Dock, press and hold it, and drag it onto the Dock

Editing mode can also be exited by tapping on the **Done** button in the top right-hand corner of the screen.

The number of items that can be added to the Dock is restricted to a maximum of four, as the icons do not resize

For older iPhones that have a physical Home button and run iOS 13, press the Home button to exit editing mode for the Dock.

Swipe up from the bottom of the screen to exit editing mode

Using the Control Center

The Control Center is a panel containing some of the most commonly-used options within the **Settings** app.

Accessing the Control Center

The Control Center can be accessed with one swipe from any screen within iOS 13, and it can also be accessed from the Lock screen. To set this up:

1 Tap once on the **Settings** app

2 Tap once on the **Control Center** tab, and drag the **Access Within Apps** button On or Off to specify if the Control Center can be accessed from there (if it is Off, it can still be accessed from any Home screen)

3 Swipe down from the top right-hand corner of any screen to access the Control Center

Control Center functionality

The Control Center contains items that have differing formats and functionality. To access these:

1 Press and hold on the folder of four icons in the top left-hand corner, to access the **Airplane Mode**, **Cellular Data**, **Wi-Fi**, **Bluetooth**, **AirDrop**, and **Personal Hotspot** options

For older iPhones that have a physical Home button and run iOS 13, access the Control Center by swiping up from the bottom of the screen.

AirDrop is the functionality for sharing items wirelessly between compatible devices. Tap once on the **AirDrop** button in the Control Center and specify whether you want to share with **Receiving Only**, **Contacts Only** or **Everyone**. Once AirDrop is set up, you can use the **Share** button in compatible apps to share items such as photos with any other AirDrop users in the vicinity.

2 Press on the **Music** button to expand the options for music controls, including playing or pausing items and changing the volume. Tap once on this icon to send music from your iPhone to other compatible devices, such as AirPod headphones or HomePods, Apple's wireless speakers

3 Tap once on individual buttons to turn items On or Off (they change color depending on their state)

4 Drag on these items to increase or decrease the screen brightness and the volume

The Control Center cannot be disabled from being accessed from the Home screen.

Hot tip

Bluetooth can be used to connect to other compatible devices, using radio waves over short distances up to approximately 20 meters. Both devices must have Bluetooth turned on and be "paired" with each other. This links them together so that content such as photos can be shared between them.

Don't forget

Press and hold on the Camera button to access options for taking a "selfie" (a self-portrait), recording a video, taking a portrait or taking a portrait selfie (see page 107).

...cont'd

Control Center controls

Access the items in the Control Center as follows:

- Tap once on this button to turn **Airplane Mode** On or Off, for network connections.

- Tap once on this button to turn **Cellular Data** On or Off, for cellular networks.

- Tap once on this button to turn **Wi-Fi** On or Off.

- Tap once on this button to turn **Bluetooth** On or Off.

- Tap once on this button to activate **AirDrop** for sharing items with other AirDrop users.

- Tap once on this button to turn **Personal Hotspot** On or Off, to use your iPhone as a hotspot for connecting another device like an iPad or Mac computer to the internet.

- Tap once on this button to **Lock** or **Unlock** screen rotation. If it is locked, the screen will not change when you change the orientation.

- Tap once on this button to turn **Do Not Disturb** mode On or Off.

- Tap once on this button to turn on the **Flashlight**. Press on the button to change the intensity of the flashlight.

- Tap once on this button to access the **Clock**, including a stopwatch and timer. Press on the button to access a scale for creating reminders.

- Tap once on this button to open the **Calculator** app.

- Tap once on this button to open the **Camera** app.

Customizing the Control Center

The Control Center can be customized so that items can be added or removed. To do this:

1 Tap once on the **Settings** app

2 Tap once on the **Control Center** tab

3 Tap once on the **Customize Controls** button

4 The items currently in the Control Center are shown at the top of the window; those that can be added are below them. Tap once on a red icon to remove an existing item, or tap once on a green icon to add new items to the Control Center

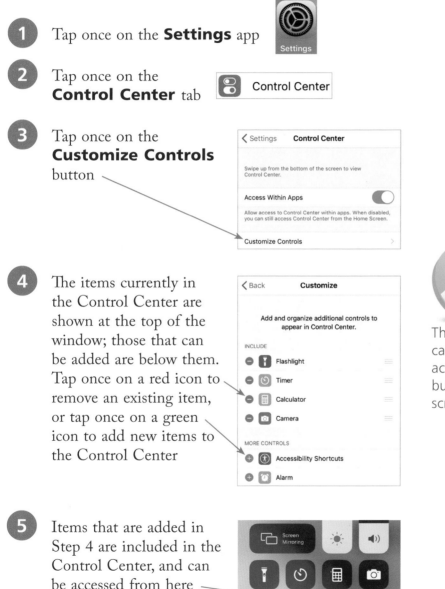

5 Items that are added in Step 4 are included in the Control Center, and can be accessed from here

Hot tip

The flashlight and the camera can both be accessed directly from buttons on the Lock screen too.

Dark Mode is a new feature in iOS 13.

Ensure the **Automatic** button is turned **Off** in Step 3 to switch between Light and Dark Mode. Use the **Automatic** option to set specific times for when Dark Mode is activated – see next page for details.

Only some of the background wallpapers (**Settings** > **Wallpaper**) work with Dark Mode. The ones that do are in the **Stills** section and are indicated by this icon on them.

Dark Mode

Being as comfortable as possible with the iPhone screen is an important factor when using it. The Display & Brightness option in the Settings app can be used to set the screen brightness and also access Night Shift for reducing the amount of blue light that is emitted by the screen. It also contains an option for Dark Mode. This inverts the screen, generally with a black background and white text. This can make the screen easier to read, particularly in the evening when the ambient light is reduced. To use Dark Mode:

1 Tap once on the **Settings** app

2 Tap once on the **Display & Brightness** tab

3 By default, **Light** is turned **On**

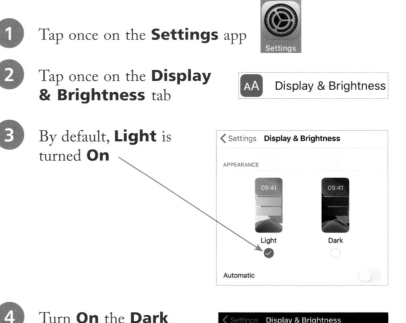

4 Turn **On** the **Dark** button. The color of the background and the text are inverted

...cont'd

Customizing Dark Mode

Dark Mode can be customized so that it is activated at specific times; e.g. at sunset. To do this:

1 Access the **Display & Brightness** option as shown on the previous page

2 Turn **On** the **Automatic** button

3 Tap once on the **Options** button

4 Tap once on the **Sunset to Sunrise** option to specify Dark Mode to be activated between these two periods

5 Tap once on the **Custom Schedule** option to set specific times for when Light Mode and Dark Mode are active

Dark Mode can also be activated by tapping on this button in the Control Center.

If the button is not visible by default in the Control Center, access **Settings > Control Center > Customize Controls** and tap once on the green button next to **Dark Mode**.

39

Setting up Siri

Siri is the iPhone's voice assistant that provides answers to a variety of verbal questions by looking at content in your iPhone and also web services. You can ask Siri questions relating to the apps on your iPhone, and also general questions such as weather conditions around the world or sports results. Initially, Siri can be set up within the **Settings** app:

1. Tap once on the **Settings** app

2. Tap once on the **Siri & Search** tab

Options for Siri

Within the Siri settings there are options for its operation:

Hot tip

Siri can be used to translate English words or phrases into different languages. More languages have been added in iOS 13, and there are now 50 different languages.

1. Drag the **Listen for "Hey Siri"** button **On** if you want to be able to access Siri just by saying **Hey Siri**

2. Make selections here for the language, voice type, feedback and your own details to use with Siri

‹ Settings	Siri & Search
ASK SIRI	
Listen for "Hey Siri"	⬤
Press Home for Siri	⬤
Allow Siri When Locked	⬤
Language	English (United States) ›
Siri Voice	American (Female) ›
Voice Feedback	Always ›
My Information	Nick Vandome ›
Siri can help you get things done just by asking. About Ask Siri & Privacy...	
SIRI SUGGESTIONS	
Suggestions in Search	⬤
Suggestions in Look Up	⬤
Suggestions on Lock Screen	⬤

3 If using "Hey Siri", it has to be set up by training it for your voice. Tap once on the **Continue** button

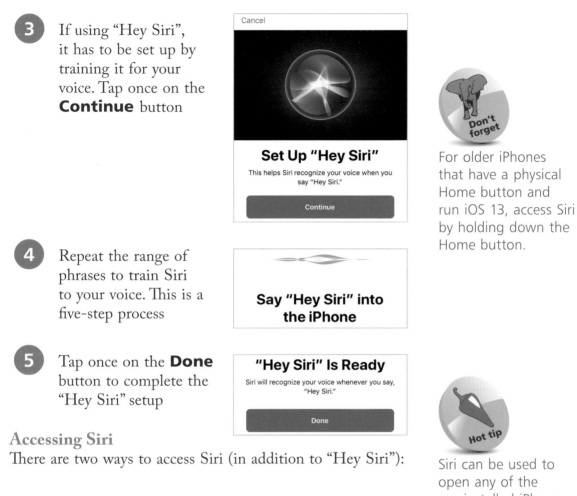

Cancel

Set Up "Hey Siri"

This helps Siri recognize your voice when you say "Hey Siri."

Continue

4 Repeat the range of phrases to train Siri to your voice. This is a five-step process

Say "Hey Siri" into the iPhone

5 Tap once on the **Done** button to complete the "Hey Siri" setup

"Hey Siri" Is Ready

Siri will recognize your voice whenever you say, "Hey Siri."

Done

Accessing Siri

There are two ways to access Siri (in addition to "Hey Siri"):

1 Press and hold the **On/Off** button until the Siri screen appears

What can I help you with?

2 Ask your question to Siri. After the reply, tap once on this icon to ask another question

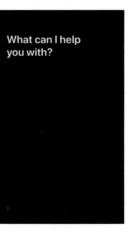

Don't forget

For older iPhones that have a physical Home button and run iOS 13, access Siri by holding down the Home button.

41

Hot tip

Siri can be used to open any of the pre-installed iPhone apps, simply by saying **Open Photos**, for example.

Finding Things with Siri

Siri is very versatile and can be used for a wide range of functions, including finding things on your iPhone, searching the web, getting weather forecasts, finding locations, and even playing music.

Accessing your apps
To use Siri to find things on your iPhone:

Siri can also display specific contacts. Say **Show me...** followed by the person's name to view their details (if they are in your contacts – see pages 70-71).

Siri can also read out your information: open an item such as calendar appointments and then say **Read appointment**.

You can ask for weather forecasts for specific periods such as **Today** or **This Week**. However, Siri's power of forecasting only stretches to 10 days in the future.

1 Access Siri as shown on page 41

2 To find something from your iPhone apps, ask a question such as **Open my contacts**

Hey Siri open my contacts

3 The requested app is displayed

Getting the weather
You can ask Siri for weather forecasts for locations around the world. Simply ask for the weather in a certain city or location.

Finding locations

Siri is also effective for viewing locations within the Maps app. This can be done on an international, national or city level. Siri can also be used to get directions.

Searching locally

If Location Services is turned On for Siri, then you can ask for local information such as **Show the nearest Indian restaurants**.

Playing music

You can use Siri to play any of the music that you have in the Music app. Simply ask Siri to play a track and it will start playing. (Music can be downloaded from the iTunes Store app; see pages 158-160 for more details.)

To stop a song, simply say **Stop playing** and the song will be paused.

Hot tip

Siri can be used with certain third-party apps to perform tasks such as booking a taxi or a restaurant table.

Don't forget

Siri can also play a whole album as well as individual tracks.

Don't forget

Items can also be searched for using the Spotlight Search option. This can be accessed by swiping downwards on the Home screen and entering a keyword or phrase in the Search box at the top of the window. Items can be searched for on your iPhone (including apps), or use the **Search Web** button at the bottom of the window to search the web.

Reachability

Because of the size of the iPhone 11, the iPhone 11 Pro, and the iPhone 11 Pro Max, it is not always easy to access all items with one hand. This is overcome by a feature known as Reachability, which can be accessed from any screen of the iPhone. This moves the items on the screen to the bottom half, and they can all be accessed from here.

Hot tip

The Reachability function is not turned On by default. To enable it, go to **Settings** > **Accessibility** > **Touch** and drag the **Reachability** button **On**, underneath the **Interaction** heading.

Don't forget

For older iPhones that have a physical Home button and run iOS 13, access Reachability by gently double-tapping the Home button, rather than double-clicking.

Hot tip

The **Display & Brightness** settings can also be used to increase the text size for supported apps. Tap once on the **Text Size** button to access a slider with which you can set the required text size.

1 By default, all items on the screen take up the whole area

2 Swipe down on the bottom edge of the screen

3 The items on the top half of the screen are moved to the bottom half

4 The Reachability effect stays in place for one action; e.g. after you tap on an item, the screen reverts to normal size

Night Shift

Getting a good night's sleep is becoming increasingly recognized as a vital and often overlooked element of our overall health and wellbeing. One of the biggest obstacles to this is the amount of artificial lighting that we experience at night time, such as street lighting, lighting in the home, and the light emitted from mobile devices such as iPhones. This type of light is known as "blue light", and it is one of the most restrictive in terms of getting a good night's sleep, as it is the type of light that instructs the body that it is time to be awake and alert. One option to reduce the impact of blue light from your iPhone is to use the Night Shift option, which reduces the amount of blue light that is emitted.

1 Tap once on the **Settings** app

Settings

2 Tap once on the **Display & Brightness** tab

AA   Display & Brightness

3 Tap once on the **Night Shift** button

Night Shift   Off >

4 Drag the **Scheduled** button **On** and tap once on the **From/To** option to set a time period for when Night Shift is applied

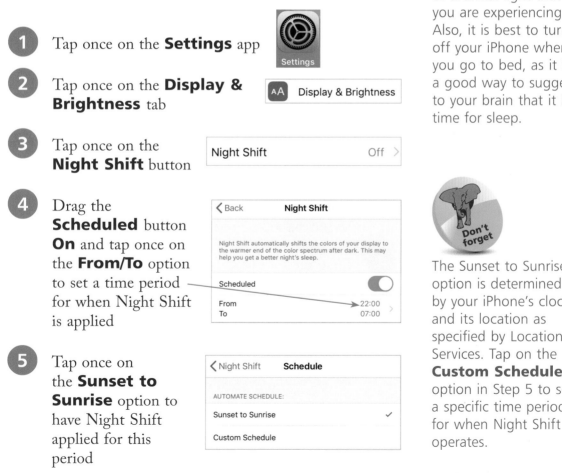

‹ Back   **Night Shift**

Night Shift automatically shifts the colors of your display to the warmer end of the color spectrum after dark. This may help you get a better night's sleep.

Scheduled   ⬤

From   22:00
To   07:00

5 Tap once on the **Sunset to Sunrise** option to have Night Shift applied for this period

‹ Night Shift   **Schedule**

AUTOMATE SCHEDULE:

Sunset to Sunrise   ✓

Custom Schedule

Beware

Try not to use your iPhone, or other mobile devices, for prolonged periods just before you go to bed, to reduce the amount of artificial light that you are experiencing. Also, it is best to turn off your iPhone when you go to bed, as it is a good way to suggest to your brain that it is time for sleep.

Don't forget

The Sunset to Sunrise option is determined by your iPhone's clock and its location as specified by Location Services. Tap on the **Custom Schedule** option in Step 5 to set a specific time period for when Night Shift operates.

Do Not Disturb

The iPhone is excellent for keeping up-to-date with calls and notifications from apps, so you never miss an important call or message. However, there can be times when constant notifications can be too intrusive, and you may wish to have a period of quiet without having to turn off notifications completely. This can be achieved with the Do Not Disturb feature. To use this:

Don't forget

Tap once on the **From/To** option in Step 4 to set the time period for Do Not Disturb.

Hot tip

The Bedtime option in Step 5 can be specified in the **Clock** app. Tap on the **Bedtime** button on the bottom toolbar and enter a time period that constitutes bedtime. The Clock app can be set to activate an alarm at the end of the bedtime period, and Do Not Disturb will apply during the bedtime hours.

1. Tap once on the **Settings** app

2. Tap once on the **Do Not Disturb** tab

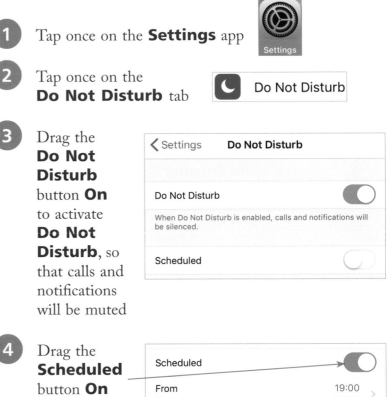

3. Drag the **Do Not Disturb** button **On** to activate **Do Not Disturb**, so that calls and notifications will be muted

4. Drag the **Scheduled** button **On** to set a specific time period for Do Not Disturb to be applied

5. Drag the **Dim Lock Screen** button **On** to darken the Lock screen and send any notifications to the Notifications Center

Using Haptic Touch

One of the features using touch on the iPhone is Haptic Touch. This can be used to activate different options for certain apps, depending on the length of the press on an item. For instance, a single press or tap can be used to open an app. However, if you press for longer (long press) on the app then different options appear in a Quick Actions menu:

Quick Actions

Quick Actions can be used to perform actions without opening an app first (this is for the Camera app):

Haptic Touch is a new feature in iOS 13, updated from what was previously known as 3D Touch.

1 Press and hold on an app until the Quick Actions menu is displayed. For the **Camera** app this includes options for taking a selfie, recording a video, taking a portrait, or taking a selfie portrait

Other apps that use Haptic Touch and Quick Actions include: Safari and Mail. In the Safari app, perform a long press on a webpage link to view a preview of the page and a Quick Actions menu. In the Mail app, perform a long press on an email in your Inbox to access options for replying to or organizing the email message.

Using Haptic Touch within apps

Haptic Touch can also be used to quickly access menus for selected items within compatible apps. To do this, using the Photos app:

1 Open the Photos app and press and hold on a photo

2 The photo is displayed, along with the Quick Actions menu with options relating to the photo

Screen Time

The amount of time that we spend on our digital devices is a growing issue in society, and steps are being taken to let us see exactly how much time we are spending looking at our cellular phone screens. In iOS 13, a range of screen-use options can be monitored with the Screen Time feature. To use this:

1 Select **Settings** > **Screen Time**

Screen Time

2 Tap once on the **Turn On Screen Time** button

‹ Settings   **Screen Time**

Turn On Screen Time

Get a weekly report with insights about your screen time and set time limits for apps you want to manage.

3 Options for using Screen Time are displayed

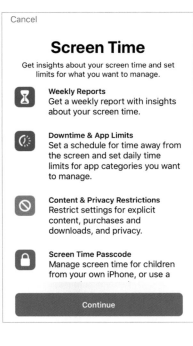

Cancel

Screen Time

Get insights about your screen time and set limits for what you want to manage.

Weekly Reports
Get a weekly report with insights about your screen time.

Downtime & App Limits
Set a schedule for time away from the screen and set daily time limits for app categories you want to manage.

Content & Privacy Restrictions
Restrict settings for explicit content, purchases and downloads, and privacy.

Screen Time Passcode
Manage screen time for children from your own iPhone, or use a

Continue

Hot tip

Once Screen Time has been turned on, it can be turned off again by tapping once on the **Turn Off Screen Time** button at the bottom of the main Screen Time window in the Settings app, as shown in Step 6 on the next page.

4 Tap once on the **Continue** button

5 Screen Time can be set up for your own use, or on a child's iPhone. If it is set up for a child, there will be more parental control options for controlling the type of content that is available. Tap once on the required option

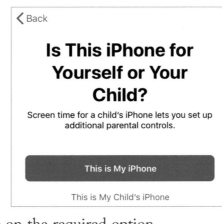

6 The current Screen Time usage is shown at the top of the Screen Time settings screen. More Screen Time options are shown below – see pages 50-51

If Screen Time is set up for a child (**This is My Child's iPhone** option in Step 5), you can create a parental passcode that is required for a child to continue using the iPhone once one of the Screen Time restrictions has been reached. (See pages 52-53 for details.)

Each week, the Screen Time option produces a report based on the overall usage, as shown in Step 6. The report is identified with a notification when it is published each week.

...cont'd

Options for Screen Time

Within the Screen Time settings there are options for viewing apps and content on your iPhone. Each of these is accessed on the main Screen Time settings page:

1 Tap once on **Downtime**

2 Drag the **Downtime** button **On** and tap once on the **Start** and **End** buttons to select times for when only specified apps are available, then return to the Screen Time settings screen

3 Tap once on **Always Allowed**

4 The apps that are always allowed to operate, regardless of what settings there are for Screen Time, are displayed. Tap once on the red circle next to one to remove it. Select items below the **Choose Apps** heading to add more

5 Tap once on **Content & Privacy Restrictions**

6 Drag the **Content & Privacy Restrictions** button **On** to apply restrictions for blocking inappropriate content (see page 53 for details)

Don't forget

Content restrictions can be applied for content from the iTunes Store (such as age ratings for movies and TV shows), web content, and search content accessed by Siri, the iPhone's digital voice assistant.

7 Return to the Screen Time settings screen, then tap once on **App Limits**

 App Limits
Set time limits for apps.

8 Tap once on the **Add Limit** button to add time limits for using types of apps

< Screen Time   **App Limits**

Set daily time limits for app categories you want to manage. App limits reset every day at midnight.

Add Limit

9 Select a category for the types of apps that you want to limit use of (or select **All Apps & Categories**)

Cancel   **Choose Apps**   Add

CATEGORIES

✓ All Apps & Categories

○ Social Networking
WhatsApp, Messages, and 2 more

○ Games

○ Entertainment
Amazon Alexa, TV, and 4 more

10 Drag here to specify a time limit for using apps within the category selected in the previous step. By default, this is for each day. Tap once on the **Customize Days** button to set different time limits for specific days

< Back   **All Apps & Categories**

Time   2 hr, 20 min

0   18
1   19
2 hours   20 min
3   21
4   22

Customize Days   >

App limits apply to all devices that are using iCloud for screen time. A notification will appear five minutes before the limit expires.

APPS & CATEGORIES

All Apps & Categories

Edit Apps

Delete Limit

Don't forget

The time limit for using apps is only a suggestion, and the apps do not stop operating when the limit is reached. Instead, a notification appears to alert you to the fact that the time limit has been reached. Tap once on the **Ignore Limit** button to continue using the app.

Time Limit
You've reached your limit on Music.
Ignore Limit

Select an option for how long you want to ignore the time limit.

Remind Me in 15 Minutes

Ignore Limit For Today

Cancel

Restrictions for Children

If children or grandchildren have access to an iPhone, this can raise genuine concerns about the type of content that they may be accessing, and also the amount of time that they spend on the device. The Screen Time options can be used to apply specific settings for a child, so that you can have a degree of control over what they are using. These are similar to the standard Screen Time options, but they can be set up with an initial selection of wizards, and it is also possible to include a parental passcode that has to be entered when limits are reached. To set up restrictions for children:

1 Access Screen Time options as shown on page 48, and tap once on the **This is My Child's iPhone** button

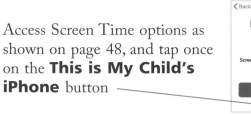

2 Select options for **Downtime**, for when the device cannot be used, by tapping on the **Start** and **End** options and specifying a time for each. Tap once on the **Set Downtime** button to apply these times

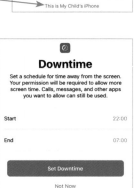

3 On the **App Limits** screen, tap once on the category of apps that you want to restrict and tap once on the **Set App Limit** button. Enter time controls as shown in Step 10 on page 51

Hot tip

Drag the **Block At End of Limit** button **On** on the App Limits page that is accessed from Step 3, to ensure that apps cannot continue to be used after the time limit unless a parental passcode is entered.

Block At End of Limit ⬤

4 On the **Content & Privacy** screen, tap once on the **Continue** button

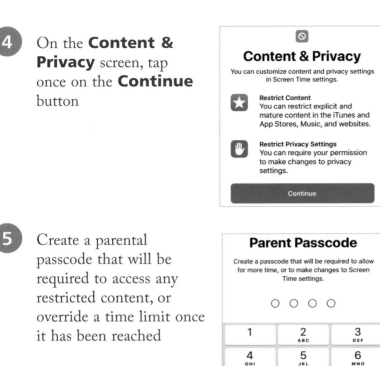

5 Create a parental passcode that will be required to access any restricted content, or override a time limit once it has been reached

6 Tap once on the **Content & Privacy Restrictions** option, as shown on page 50. Drag the **Content & Privacy Restrictions** button **On** to access the available options. These include options for limiting **iTunes & App Store Purchases**, specifying **Allowed Apps**, and selecting **Content Restrictions** for media such as movies, TV shows, music, and books that have been downloaded from the iTunes Store

A passcode can also be created for your own Screen Time settings. This prevents anyone else from changing these settings, and can be used to allow more time once a time limit is reached.

If you are setting restrictions for a child or a grandchild, tell them about it and explain what you are doing and why.

About Apple Pay

Apple Pay is Apple's service for mobile, contactless payment. It can be used by adding credit, debit, and store cards to your iPhone via the Wallet app, and then paying for items by using your Face ID (or Touch ID for older iPhones) as authorization for payment. Credit, debit, and store cards have to be issued by banks or retailers that support Apple Pay, and there are an increasing number that do so, with more joining on a regular basis. Outlets also have to support Apple Pay but this, too, is increasing and, given the success of the iPhone, is likely to grow at a steady rate.

Setting up Apple Pay

To use Apple Pay you have to first add your cards to your iPhone (and be signed in to iCloud):

At the time of printing, Apple Pay has no limit for in-store purchases in the US and the UK.

Cards can also be added to the Wallet at any time from **Settings** > **Wallet & Apple Pay** > **Add Card**. This can also be used to create cash payments to people, using the Messages app. See page 99 for details.

If your bank does not yet support Apple Pay then you will not be able to add your credit or debit card details to the Wallet app.

1 Tap once on the **Wallet** app

2 Tap once on the **Add Credit or Debit Card** link, or tap once on this button

3 Tap once on the **Continue** button

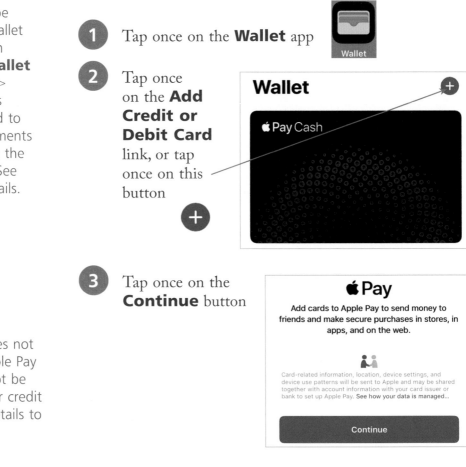

4 The card details can be added to the Wallet app by taking a photo of the card. Place the card on a flat surface, and position it within the white box. The card number is then added automatically. Alternatively, tap once on **Enter Card Details Manually**

Add Card

Position your card in the frame.

Enter Card Details Manually

Beware

Obtaining your card number using the camera is not always completely accurate. Take the photo in good light, always check the number afterwards, and amend it if necessary.

5 Once the card details have been added, your bank or store card issuer has to verify your card. This can be done either by a text message or a phone call

6 Once the Apple Pay wizard is completed, details of the card appear in the Wallet app

FROM SANTANDER

"Santander Debit Card" is ready for Apple Pay.

Don't forget

Although no form of contactless payment is 100% secure, Apple Pay does offer some security safeguards. One is that no card information is passed between the retailer and the user; the transaction is done by sending an encrypted token that is used to authorize the payment. Also, the use of the Face ID process ensures another step of authorization that is not available with all other forms of contactless payment.

7 To pay for items with Apple Pay, open the **Wallet** app and tap once on the card you want to use. Hold your iPhone up to the contactless payment card reader. Press the **On/Off** button twice and look at the phone screen to authorize the payment with Face ID. (Retailers must have a contactless card reader in order for Apple Pay to be used)

Face ID

Beware

There is no separate headphone jack on the iPhone. Instead, headphones are connected via the Lightning Connector jack. However, this means that earphones and headphones with a traditional jack will not work with the iPhone, unless the Lightning to 3.5mm headphone jack adapter is used (this is not included with the iPhone).

Don't forget

All models of the iPhone can be used with AirPods, the wireless headphones from Apple.

Using the EarPods

The iPhone EarPods are not only an excellent way to listen to music and other audio on your iPhone; they can also be used in a variety of ways with the phone function:

The EarPods contain three main controls:

Down volume   Up volume

Central control button

- Plug in the EarPods to use them to hear someone who is calling you. Speak normally, and the other person will be able to hear you via the EarPods' in-built microphone.

- Click once in the middle of the control button to answer an incoming call.

- Press and hold in the middle of the control button for a couple of seconds (until you hear two beeps) to decline an incoming call.

- Click once in the middle of the control button to end the current call.

- If you are on a call and receive another one, click once in the middle of the control button to put the first call on hold and activate the second call.

- Press and hold the middle of the control button to dial a number using Voice Control, whereby you can speak the required number.

- Click on the control button when playing a music track to pause it. Click again to restart it. Double-click on the control button to move to the next track. Triple-click on the control button to move back to the previous track.

3 Head in the iCloud

iCloud, the online storage service, is at the heart of the iPhone for backing up your content and sharing it with other family members.

It is free to register for and set up a standard iCloud account.

An Apple ID can be created with an email address and password. It can then be used to access a variety of services, including the iTunes Store, Books, and the App Store.

To access your iCloud account through the website, access www.icloud.com and enter your Apple ID details.

What is iCloud?

iCloud is the Apple online storage and backup service that performs a number of valuable functions:

- It makes your content available across multiple devices. The content is stored in the iCloud and then pushed out to other iCloud-enabled devices, including the iPad, iPod Touch, and other Mac or Windows computers.

- It enables online access to your content via the iCloud website. This includes your iCloud email, photos, contacts, calendar, reminders, and documents.

- It can back up the content on your iPhone.

To use iCloud you must have an Apple ID. This can be done when you first set up your iPhone, or at a later date. Once you have registered for and set up iCloud, it works automatically so you do not have to worry about anything.

1. Tap once on the **Settings** app

2. At the top of the Settings panel, tap once on the **Sign in to your iPhone** option

3. If you already have an Apple ID, enter your details and tap once on the **Sign In** button

4. If you do not yet have an Apple ID, tap once on the **Don't have an Apple ID or forgot it?** link and follow the steps to create your Apple ID

iCloud Settings

Once you have set up your iCloud account, you can then apply settings for how it works. Once you have done this, you will not have to worry about it again:

1 Tap once on the **Apple ID** section in the Settings app

2 Tap once on the **iCloud** button

3 Drag these buttons **On** for each item that you wish to be included in iCloud. Each item is then saved and stored in the iCloud and made available to your other iCloud-enabled devices

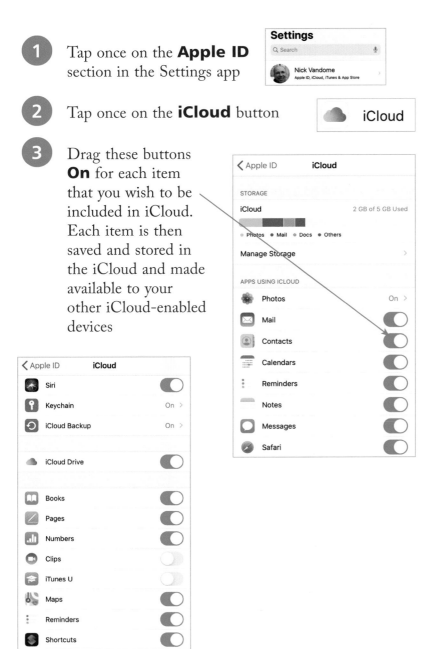

Adding iCloud Storage

By default, you get 5GB of free storage space with an iCloud account. However, you can upgrade this if you want to increase the amount of storage. To do this:

Hot tip

If you have a lot of photos stored in iCloud then you may want to consider increasing your amount of storage.

1 Access **iCloud** in Settings, as shown on page 59

☁ iCloud

2 Tap once on the **Manage Storage** button to view how your iCloud storage is being used

< Apple ID   **iCloud**

STORAGE

iCloud   2 GB of 5 GB Used

● Photos ● Mail ● Docs ● Others

Manage Storage   >

3 Tap once on the **Change Storage Plan** button if you want to change the amount of iCloud storage

< iCloud   **iCloud Storage**

iCloud   2 GB of 5 GB Used

● Photos ● Mail ● Docs ● Others

Change Storage Plan   5 GB >

4 Tap once on one of the storage options to buy this amount of iCloud storage. (Note: charges appear in your local currency.) Tap once on the amount of storage you require, to complete the change of storage

Back   **Upgrade iCloud Storage**   Buy

iCloud stores the most important things from your device, like photos, documents, contacts, and more, so they're always available, even if you lose your device.

CURRENT PLAN

5GB   Free   ✓

CHOOSE UPGRADE

50GB   £0.79 per month

200GB   £2.49 per month
        Can be shared with your family

Backing up with iCloud

All of the items that you have assigned to iCloud
(see page 59) should be backed up there automatically.
However, if this is not happening you may need to turn on
the iCloud Backup. To do this:

1 Within the
iCloud section
of the Settings app,
tap once on the **iCloud Backup** button, if it is **Off**

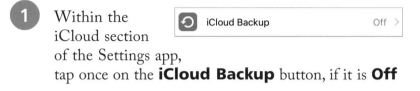

2 The iCloud
Backup button
will be **Off**

> ‹ iCloud **Backup**
>
> BACKUP
>
> iCloud Backup
>
> Automatically back up data such as your photo library,
> accounts, documents, Home configuration, and settings
> when this iPhone is plugged in, locked, and connected to
> Wi-Fi. Learn more...

3 Drag the **iCloud Backup** button **On** to enable
automatic backup for iCloud. This has to be done
over Wi-Fi, with the iPhone locked and plugged in

> ‹ iCloud **Backup**
>
> BACKUP
>
> iCloud Backup
>
> Automatically back up data such as your photo library,
> accounts, documents, Home configuration, and settings
> when this iPhone is plugged in, locked, and connected to
> Wi-Fi. Learn more...
>
> Back Up Now
>
> iCloud Backup will occur later when plugged-in, locked,
> and connected to Wi-Fi.

4 You can also back up manually at any time by
tapping once on the **Back Up Now** button

Another useful iCloud
function is the iCloud
Keychain (**Settings** >
Apple ID > **iCloud**
> **Keychain**). If this
is enabled, it can keep
all of your passwords
and credit card
information up-to-
date across multiple
devices and remember
them when you use
them on websites.
The information
is encrypted and
controlled through
your Apple ID.

61

About Family Sharing

As everyone gets more and more digital devices it is becoming increasingly important to be able to share content with other people, particularly family members. In iOS 13, the Family Sharing function enables you to share items that you have downloaded from the App Store, such as music and movies, with up to six other family members, as long as they have an Apple ID Account. Once this has been set up, it is also possible to share items such as family calendars and photos, and even see where family members are on a map. To set up and start using Family Sharing:

Beware

To use Family Sharing, the other members of the group need to have iOS 8 (or later) installed on their mobile devices, or OS X Yosemite (or later) on an Apple desktop or laptop computer.

1 Access the Apple ID section within the Settings app, as shown on page 59

2 Tap once on the **Set Up Family Sharing...** link

3 Tap once on the **Get Started** button

4 Tap once on the first item you want to share via Family Sharing. This includes music, iCloud storage plans, iTunes and App Store purchases, and location sharing for finding a lost or stolen Apple device

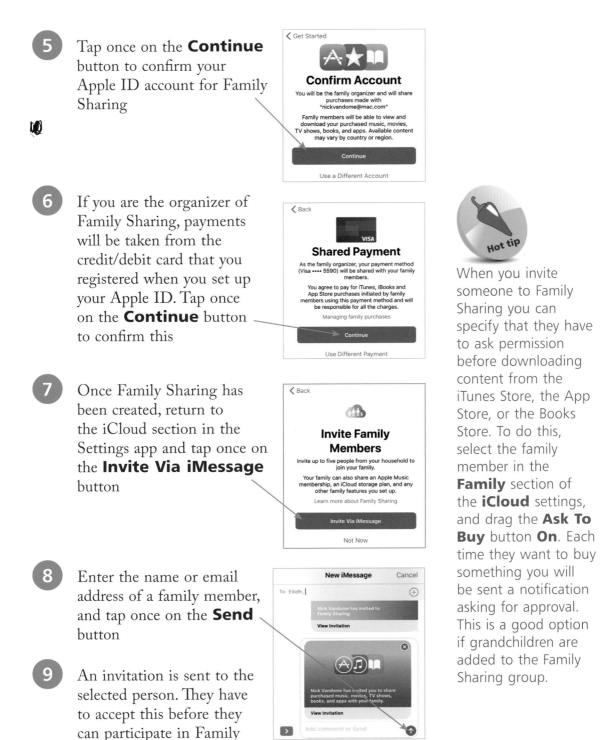

5 Tap once on the **Continue** button to confirm your Apple ID account for Family Sharing

6 If you are the organizer of Family Sharing, payments will be taken from the credit/debit card that you registered when you set up your Apple ID. Tap once on the **Continue** button to confirm this

7 Once Family Sharing has been created, return to the iCloud section in the Settings app and tap once on the **Invite Via iMessage** button

8 Enter the name or email address of a family member, and tap once on the **Send** button

9 An invitation is sent to the selected person. They have to accept this before they can participate in Family Sharing

Hot tip

When you invite someone to Family Sharing you can specify that they have to ask permission before downloading content from the iTunes Store, the App Store, or the Books Store. To do this, select the family member in the **Family** section of the **iCloud** settings, and drag the **Ask To Buy** button **On**. Each time they want to buy something you will be sent a notification asking for approval. This is a good option if grandchildren are added to the Family Sharing group.

Using Family Sharing

Once you have set up Family Sharing and added family members, you can start sharing a selection of items.

Sharing photos

Photos can be shared with Family Sharing, with the Family album that is created automatically within the Photos app.

Beware

Photo Sharing has to be turned **On** to enable Family Sharing for photos (**Settings > Photos > Shared Albums**).

Hot tip

When someone else in your Family Sharing circle adds a photo to the Family album, you are notified in the Notification Center and also by a red notification on the Photos app.

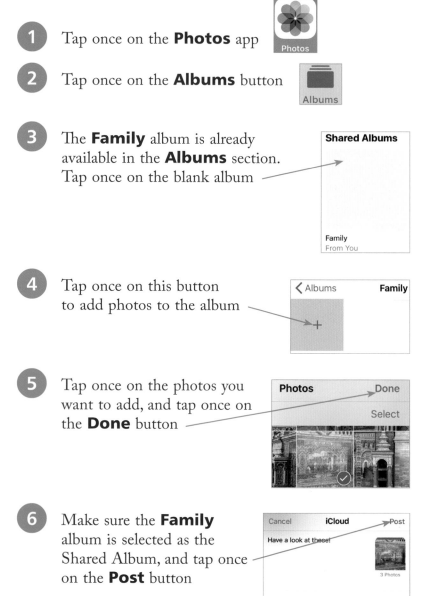

1 Tap once on the **Photos** app

2 Tap once on the **Albums** button

3 The **Family** album is already available in the **Albums** section. Tap once on the blank album

4 Tap once on this button to add photos to the album

5 Tap once on the photos you want to add, and tap once on the **Done** button

6 Make sure the **Family** album is selected as the Shared Album, and tap once on the **Post** button

Sharing calendars

Family Sharing also generates a Family calendar that can be used by all Family Sharing members:

1 Tap once on the **Calendar** app

2 Tap once on this button to create a New Event. The current calendar will probably not be the Family one. Tap once on the calendar name to change it

3 Tap once on the **Family** calendar

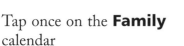

4 The **Family** calendar is now selected for the event

Calendar	● Family >

5 Complete the details for the event. It will be added to your calendar, with the **Family** tag. Other people in your Family Sharing circle will have this event added to their Family calendar too, and they will be sent a notification

19:00	Fancy dress party
	Edinburgh
20:00	
21:00	
22:00	
23:00	
00:00	
Today	Calendars Inbox

Don't forget

When someone in the Family Sharing circle adds an event to the Family calendar it will appear in your calendar with the appropriate tag. A red notification will also appear on the Calendar app, and it will appear in the Notification Center (if the Calendar has been selected to appear here).

65

...cont'd

Finding family members

Family Sharing makes it easy to keep in touch with the rest of the family and see exactly where they are. This can be done with the Find My app. The other person must have their iPhone (or other Apple device) turned on, be online and be sharing their location. To do this:

1 Tap once on the **Find My** app

2 Your own location has to be shared if you want other people to see it. Tap once on the **Me** button at the bottom of the window, and drag the **Share My Location** button **On**

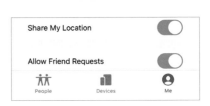

3 The details of any people who are linked via your Family Sharing are displayed. Tap once on a person's name to view their details and location in the top panel (if they are online and have shared their location on their device)

Don't forget

Tap once on your own name at the bottom-left of the screen to see your settings in the Find My app. This is where you can share your location. Share My Location also has to be turned on within **Settings** > **Privacy** > **Location Services** > **Share My Location**.

Me

Sharing apps, music, books and movies

Family Sharing means that all members of the group can share purchases from the iTunes Store, the App Store, or the Books store. To do this:

1 Open either **App Store**, **iTunes Store**, or **Books**

2 For the **App Store**: tap once on the Account icon and tap once on the **Purchased** button

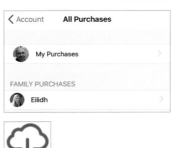

Using Family Sharing, other members of the group will be able to access and download the content that you have purchased, too.

or

for the **iTunes Store**: tap once on the **More** button on the bottom toolbar and tap once on the **Purchased** button

or

for **Books**: tap once on the Account icon

3 For all three apps, tap once on a member under **Family Purchases** to view their purchases and download them, if required, by tapping once on this button

iCloud Drive and the Files App

One of the features of iCloud is the iCloud Drive, which can be used to store documents such as those created with the Apple suite of productivity apps (available in the App Store): Pages (word processing), Numbers (spreadsheets), and Keynote (presentations). These documents can then be accessed with the Files app.

Hot tip

The Files app can also be used with other online storage services such as Dropbox and Google Drive, if you have one of these accounts. If so, they will appear under the **Locations** section in Step 3.

Hot tip

Tap once on the **Select** button at the top of any open folder, and tap once on an item to select it. Then use these buttons to, from left to right: share the selected item; duplicate an item; move an item; or delete an item.

1. Access the **iCloud** settings as shown on page 59, and drag the **iCloud Drive** button **On**. Drag **On** the buttons for any compatible apps that you want to use with iCloud Drive

2. Tap once on the **Files** app

3. Tap once on the **iCloud Drive** button to view its contents

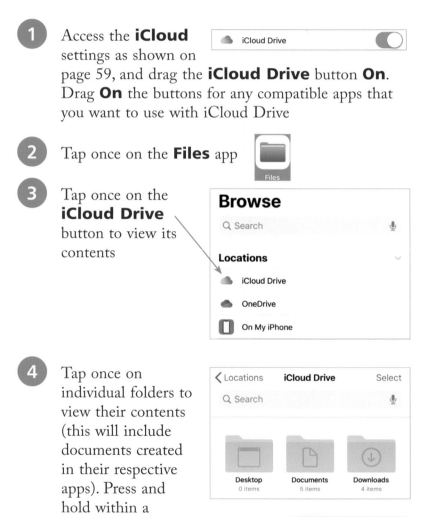

4. Tap once on individual folders to view their contents (this will include documents created in their respective apps). Press and hold within a location and tap once on the **New Folder** button to create a new folder for content

(4) Calls and Contacts

One of the main uses for the iPhone is still to make and receive phone calls. This chapter shows what you need for this.

Adding Contacts

Because of its power and versatility, it is sometimes forgotten that one of the reasons for the iPhone's existence is to make phone calls. Before you start doing this, it is a good idea to add family and friends to the Contacts app. This will enable you to phone them without having to tap in their phone number each time. To add a contact:

1 Tap once on the **Contacts** app

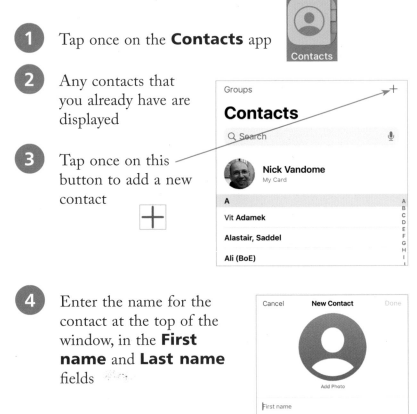

2 Any contacts that you already have are displayed

3 Tap once on this button to add a new contact

4 Enter the name for the contact at the top of the window, in the **First name** and **Last name** fields

Don't forget

Tap once on the green button next to a field to add another field. Tap once on a red button to delete a field.

5 Tap once in one of the Phone fields, or tap once on the **add phone** button to add a new Phone field

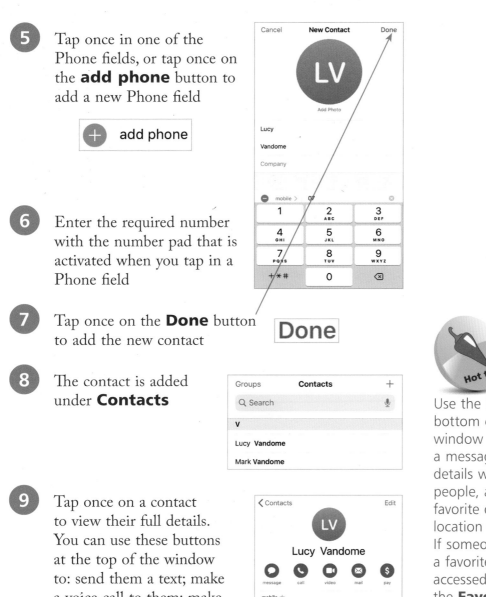

6 Enter the required number with the number pad that is activated when you tap in a Phone field

7 Tap once on the **Done** button to add the new contact

8 The contact is added under **Contacts**

9 Tap once on a contact to view their full details. You can use these buttons at the top of the window to: send them a text; make a voice call to them; make a video call; send them an email (if their email address is included); or send them money via Apple Pay (if this is available)

Hot tip

Use the buttons at the bottom of a contact's window to send them a message, share their details with other people, add them as a favorite or share your location with them. If someone is added as a favorite, they can be accessed directly from the **Favorites** button on the bottom toolbar of the **Phone** app.

Making a Call

The iPhone can be used to make calls to specific phone numbers that you enter manually, or to contacts in your Contacts app.

Dialing a number

To make a call by dialing a specific number, first tap once on the **Phone** app.

You must have a SIM card inserted in your iPhone and an appropriate cellular/mobile service provider in order to make a call with the **Phone** app, unless it is through an app that uses Wi-Fi, such as FaceTime – see pages 126-127.

 1 Tap once on the **Keypad** button at the bottom of the window

Tap once on the **Voicemail** button on the bottom toolbar to view any messages here. If you have any, there will be a red notification icon on the Voicemail button.

2 Tap on the numbers on the keypad to enter the number, which appears at the top of the window. Tap on this button to delete a number that has been entered

3 Tap once on this button to make the call

Calling a contact

To call someone who has been added to the Contacts app:

1 Open the **Phone** app, and tap once on the **Contacts** button at the bottom of the window. The Contacts app opens, with the Phone toolbar still visible at the bottom of the window

Contacts

Hot tip

To find someone in the Contacts app (either directly from the app, or from the **Contacts** button in the Phone app), swipe up and down on the screen; enter a name in the Search box at the top of the window; or tap on a letter on the alphabetic list down the right-hand side.

2 Tap once on a contact

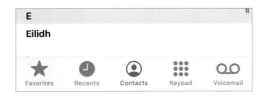

3 The full details for the contact are displayed. Tap once on the **call** button at the top of the window to call the number of the contact

call

73

Receiving a Call

When you receive a call, there are four main options:

When a call is connected, the following buttons appear on the screen. Use them to: mute a call; access the keypad again, in case you need to add any more information such as for an automated call; access the speaker so you do not have to keep the phone at your ear; add another call to create a conference call; make a FaceTime call to the caller (if they have this facility); or access your Contacts app.

1 When you receive a call, the person's name and photo (if they have been added to your Contacts) or number appears at the top of the screen

2 Tap once on the **Accept** button (or if the phone is locked, drag the **slide to answer** button to the right) to take the call

3 Tap once on the **Decline** button to decline the call, without any other actions. If the phone is locked when a call comes in, press the phone's **On/Off** button to decline the call. This is then displayed at the top of the window

4 Tap once on the **Remind Me** button to decline the call but set a reminder for yourself that the person has called

5 Select an option for when you want to be reminded

Remind Me Later

When I leave

In 1 hour

Cancel

The reminder in Step 5 will appear on the Lock screen and also as a notification in the Notification Center (if this has been specified).

6 Tap once on the **Message** button to decline the call but send the person a text message instead

7 Tap once on the text message that you want to send

Respond with:

Sorry, I can't talk right now.

I'm on my way.

Can I call you later?

Custom...

Cancel

Tap once on this button to end a call.

Saving Phone Contacts

Another quick way to add a contact is to ask someone to phone you so that you can then copy their number directly from your phone to your Contacts. You do not even have to answer the phone to do this.

Information from a caller can also be added to an existing contact. For instance, if one of your contacts calls you from a different phone, these details can be added to their existing information. To do this, tap once on the **Add to Existing Contact** button in Step 5.

1 Once someone has phoned, tap once on the **Phone** app

2 Tap once on the **Recents** button at the bottom of the window

3 The call will be displayed. Tap once on the **i** symbol

	All	Missed	Edit

014
United Kingdom   8/21/19 (i)

4 Information about the call is displayed, including the number

5 Tap once on the **Create New Contact** button

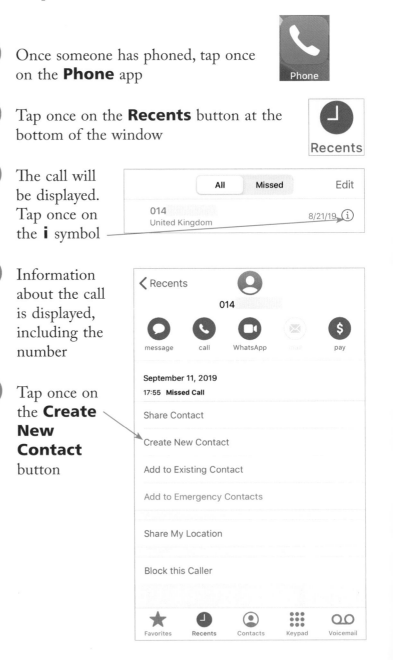

‹ Recents

014

message   call   WhatsApp   mail   pay

September 11, 2019
17:55 **Missed Call**

Share Contact

Create New Contact

Add to Existing Contact

Add to Emergency Contacts

Share My Location

Block this Caller

Favorites   Recents   Contacts   Keypad   Voicemail

To block a number from contacting you, tap once on the **Block this Caller** button in Step 5.

Block this Caller

6 The **New Contact** window opens, with the number already pre-inserted

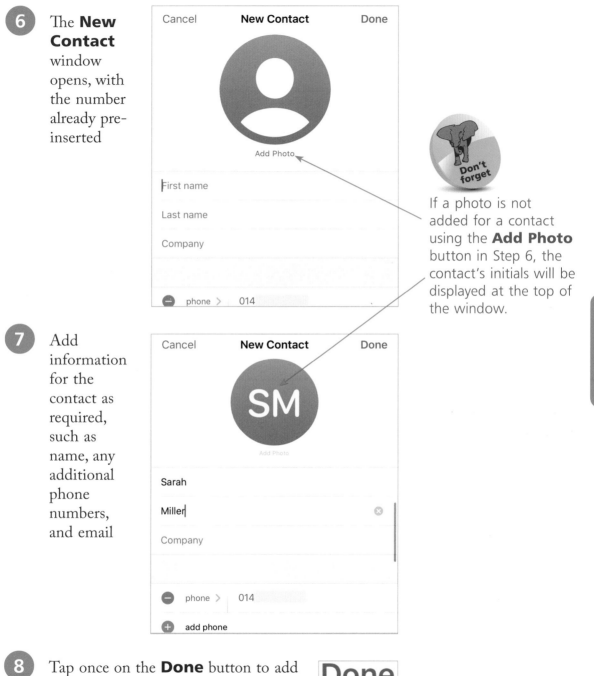

If a photo is not added for a contact using the **Add Photo** button in Step 6, the contact's initials will be displayed at the top of the window.

7 Add information for the contact as required, such as name, any additional phone numbers, and email

8 Tap once on the **Done** button to add the new contact

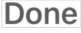

Setting Ringtones

Ringtones were one of the original "killer apps" for mobile/cell phones: the must-have accessory that helped transform the way people looked at these devices. The iPhone has a range of ringtones that can be used, and you can also download and install thousands more. To use the default ringtones:

Hot tip

Tap once on the **Tone Store** button in the Ringtone window to go to the iTunes Store, where you can download more ringtones, from the **Tones** button.

Tone Store

Don't forget

If the Ringer button on the side of the iPhone is turned Off, the iPhone can still be set to vibrate if a call or notification is received, using the **Vibrate on Silent** button at the top of the main Sounds & Haptics window (drag the button **On**).

1 Tap once on the **Settings** app

2 Tap once on the **Sounds & Haptics** tab

Sounds & Haptics

3 Tap once on the **Ringtone** link under **Sounds and Vibration Patterns** to select ringtones for when you receive a phone call

SOUNDS AND VIBRATION PATTERNS

Ringtone   Reflection >

4 Tap once on one of the options to hear a preview and select it

RINGTONES

Reflection (Default)

Apex

Beacon

✓ Bulletin

5 Sounds and vibrations can also be selected for a range of other items such as text messages, email, and calendar and reminder alerts, by going back to the Sounds and Vibration Patterns section and choosing a tone for each item

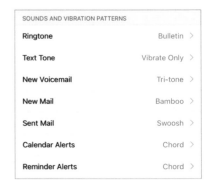

SOUNDS AND VIBRATION PATTERNS	
Ringtone	Bulletin >
Text Tone	Vibrate Only >
New Voicemail	Tri-tone >
New Mail	Bamboo >
Sent Mail	Swoosh >
Calendar Alerts	Chord >
Reminder Alerts	Chord >

Adding individual ringtones

It is also possible to set ringtones for individual people, so that you know immediately who a call is from.

1 Select a contact in the Contacts app, and tap on the **Edit** button

‹ Contacts   Edit

Eilidh

message   call   video   mail   pay

Only set ringtones for your most regular contacts, otherwise you may end up with too many variations.

2 Tap once on the **Ringtone** button

+ add email

Ringtone   Default   ›

Text Tone   Default   ›

If you are going to be using your iPhone around other people, consider turning the **Keyboard Clicks** option (at the bottom of the main **Sounds & Haptics** Settings window) to **Off**, as the noise can get annoying for those in the vicinity.

3 Tap once on a ringtone to assign this to the contact

RINGTONES

Reflection

Apex

Beacon

✓ Bulletin

By The Seaside

Phone Settings

As with most of the iPhone functions, there is a range of settings for the phone itself. To use them:

Don't forget

Use the settings for **Cellular** (**Mobile**) settings for items specific to your phone service provider.

Drag the **Silence Unknown Callers** button to **On** in Step 3 to ensure that any calls from numbers that you do not recognize (those not in your Contacts) are silenced; i.e. the phone will not ring. This is a new feature in iOS 13.

| Silence Unknown Callers | ○ |

1 Tap once on the **Settings** app

Settings

2 Tap once on the **Phone** tab

Phone

3 The Phone settings have options for responding with a text to a call that you do not take; call forwarding; call waiting; and viewing blocked callers

‹ Settings	**Phone**
My Number	+44 7957 146274 ›
CALLS	
Announce Calls	Never ›
SMS/Call Reporting	›
Wi-Fi Calling	Off ›
Calls on Other Devices	When Nearby ›
Respond with Text	›
Call Forwarding	›
Call Waiting	›
Show My Caller ID	›
CALL SILENCING AND BLOCKED CONTACTS	
Silence Unknown Callers	⬤

Calls from unknown numbers will be silenced, sent to voicemail, and displayed on the Recents list.

Incoming calls will continue to ring from people in your contacts, recent outgoing calls, and Siri Suggestions.

| Blocked Contacts | › |

4 Tap once on the **Respond with Text** button to create a text message that can be sent if you do not want to answer a call when it is received

‹ Phone	**Respond with Text**
RESPOND WITH:	
Sorry, I can't talk right now.	
I'm on my way.	
Can I call you later?	

These quick responses will be available when you respond to an incoming call with a text. Change them to say anything you like.

5 Typing and Texts

This chapter shows how to use the iPhone keyboard to add text, and also shows the range of items that can be added to messages with iOS 13, including animated Animojis and Memojis.

The iPhone Keyboard

The keyboard on the iPhone is a virtual one; i.e. it appears on the touchscreen whenever text or numbered input is required for an app. This can be for a variety of reasons:

- Entering text with a word processing app, or into an email or an organizing app such as Notes.

- Entering a web address in a web browser such as the Safari app.

- Entering information into an online form.

- Entering a password.

Viewing the keyboard

When you attempt one of the actions above, the keyboard appears so that you can enter any text or numbers:

Space bar

Shift button

Around the keyboard

To access the various keyboard controls:

1 Tap once on the **Shift** button to create a **Cap** (capital) text letter

2 Double-tap on the **Shift** button to enable **Caps Lock**

3 Tap once on this button to back-delete an item

In some apps such as Notes, Mail and Messages, it is possible to change the keyboard into a trackpad for moving the cursor. To do this, press and hold firmly on the keyboard, and then swipe over the trackpad to move the cursor around.

It is possible to increase the size of view of the iPhone keyboard with the **Zoom** feature within the Accessibility settings. See pages 182-183 for details.

To return from Caps Lock, tap once on the **Caps** button.

4 Tap once on this button to access the **Numbers** keyboard option

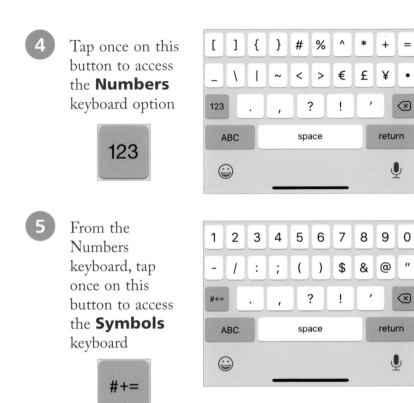

123

5 From the Numbers keyboard, tap once on this button to access the **Symbols** keyboard

#+=

Hot tip

If you are entering a password, or details into a form, the keyboard will have a **Go** or **Send** button that can be used to activate the information that has been entered.

6 Tap once on this button on either of the two keyboards above to return to the standard QWERTY option

ABC

Shortcut keys

Instead of having to go to a different keyboard every time you want to add punctuation (or numbers), there is a shortcut for this:

1 Press and hold on the **Numbers** button, and swipe over the item you want to include. This will be added, and you will remain on the QWERTY keyboard

Hot tip

Several keys have additional options that can be accessed by pressing and holding on the key. A lot of these are letters that have accented versions in different languages; e.g. a, e, i, o and u. Swipe across a letter to add it.

83

Keyboard Settings

Settings for the keyboard can be determined in the General section of the Settings app. To do this:

Hot tip

Drag the **Predictive** button **On** to enable predictive texting (see pages 86-87). Drag the **Character Preview** button **On** to show a magnified example of a letter or symbol when it is pressed, to ensure that the correct one is selected.

Hot tip

The Auto-Correction function works as you type a word, so it may change a number of times depending on the length of the word you are typing.

1 Tap once on the **Settings** app

2 Tap once on the **General** tab General

3 Tap once on the **Keyboard** link **Keyboard**

4 Drag the **Auto-Capitalization** button **On** to automatically capitalize letters at the beginning of a sentence

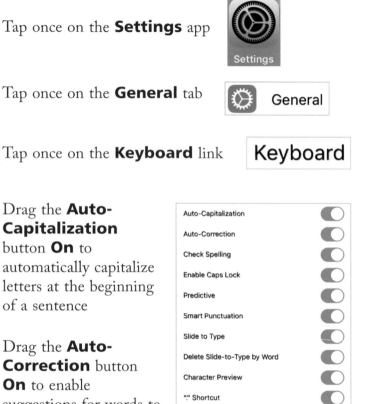

5 Drag the **Auto-Correction** button **On** to enable suggestions for words to appear as you type, particularly if you have mistyped a word

6 Drag the **Check Spelling** and **Smart Punctuation** buttons **On** to identify misspelled words (highlighted) and add punctuation

7 Drag the **Enable Caps Lock** button **On** to enable this function to be performed

8 Drag the **"." Shortcut** button **On** to add a period (full stop) and a space to start a new sentence by just tapping the space bar twice

84

9 Tap once on the **Text Replacement** link to view existing text shortcuts and also to create new ones

‹ General	**Keyboards**	
Keyboards		2 ›
Text Replacement		›

10 Tap once on this button to create new shortcuts

‹ Keyboards **Text Replacement** +

🔍 Search 🎤

A
aa 😊 xxx
J
jh Just heading off
M
mnn My name is Nick

Hot tip

With iOS 13, third-party keyboards can be downloaded from the App Store and used instead of the default one. One to look at is SwiftKey Keyboard.

11 Enter a phrase and the shortcut you want to use to create it when you type. Tap once on the **Save** button

‹ Back	**Text Replacement**	Save
Phrase	See you later	
Shortcut	syl	

12 Tap once on the **Keyboards** button in Step 9 to add a new keyboard

13 Tap once on the **Add New Keyboard...** button

Add New Keyboard...

14 Tap once on a keyboard to add it. The keyboard will be available by selecting the globe icon (see the Don't forget tip)

Cancel	**Add New Keyboard**
SUGGESTED KEYBOARDS	
English (United States)	
OTHER IPHONE KEYBOARDS	
English (Australia)	
English (Canada)	
English (India)	

Don't forget

By default, two keyboards are installed: one for the language of your region, and the emoji one. If more keyboards are added, this symbol will appear on the keyboard. Press on it to select another keyboard from the one being used. If only the two default keyboards are installed, this symbol will be the emoji one.

Using Predictive Text

Predictive text tries to guess what you are typing, and also predicts the next word following the one you have just typed. It is excellent for text messaging. To use it:

1 Tap once on the **General** tab in the Settings app

2 Tap once on the **Keyboard** link

Keyboard   >

3 Drag the **Predictive** button **On**

Predictive

4 When predictive text is activated, the QuickType bar is displayed above the keyboard. Initially, this has a suggestion for the first word to include. Tap on a word or start typing

5 As you type, suggestions appear. Tap on one to accept it. Tap on the word within the quotation marks to accept exactly what you have typed

Don't forget

Predictive text learns from your writing style as you write, and so gets more accurate at predicting words. It can also recognize a change in style for different apps such as Mail and Messages.

6 If you continue typing, the predictive suggestions will change as you add more letters

7 After you have typed a word, a suggestion for the next word appears. Tap on one of the suggestions or start typing a new word, which will then also have predictive suggestions as you type

Toggling predictive text from the keyboard
You can also toggle predictive text On or Off from the keyboard. To do this:

1 Press and hold on this button on the keyboard

2 Tap once on the **Keyboard Settings...** button to access the **Predictive** setting, from where it can be turned **On** or **Off**

It is also possible to create text by swiping over letters on the keyboard. This is known as QuickPath Typing. To set this up, access **Settings > General > Keyboard** and turn **Slide to Type** to **On**. Text can then be created by sliding your fingers over the required letters, rather than tapping on them individually. This is a new feature in iOS 13.

Slide to Type ⬤

Hot tip

Tapping the button in Step 1 allows you to add emojis, which are symbols used in text messages to signify happiness, surprise, sadness, etc. (See page 94 for details.)

One Handed Keyboard

When typing with the iPhone, this is frequently done with one hand. To make this easier, there is an option for formatting the keyboard for one handed typing. To do this:

Beware

When using your iPhone one handed, make sure you keep a good hold on it so that it does not fall on the ground.

1 Open the **General** tab in the Settings app, and tap once on the **One Handed Keyboard** link

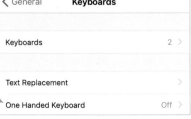

2 Select the **Left** or **Right** option for the keyboard

3 If more than one keyboard has been added (e.g. the emoji keyboard), press and hold on this button on the keyboard, and tap once on the options for moving the keyboard to the left or right

4 The keyboard is moved into the position selected in either Steps 2 or 3. Tap once here to revert to the original keyboard

Entering Text

Once you have applied the keyboard settings that you require, you can start entering text. To do this:

1 Tap once on the screen to activate the keyboard from the app. Start typing with the keyboard. The text will appear at the point where you tapped on the screen

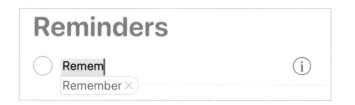

2 As you type, Auto-Correction comes up with suggestions (if it is turned On). Tap once on the space bar to accept the suggestion, or tap once on the cross next to it to reject it

3 If Check Spelling is enabled in the keyboard settings, any misspelled words appear highlighted. Press on the word to access a replacement word. Tap once on the replacement to use it, if required

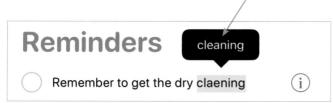

4 Double-tap the space bar to enter a period (full stop) and a space at the end of a sentence

Don't forget

If you keep typing as normal, the Auto-Correction suggestion will disappear when you finish the word.

Don't forget

If Predictive text is turned **On** (**Settings** > **General** > **Keyboard** > **Predictive**), the Auto-Correction suggestions will appear on the QuickType bar above the keyboard, rather than below the word being typed, as in Step 1.

Don't forget

The **"."** **Shortcut** option has to be turned **On** (**Settings** > **General** > **Keyboard** > **"."** **Shortcut**) for the functionality in Step 4 to work (see page 84).

Editing Text

Once text has been entered it can be selected, copied, cut, and pasted. Depending on the app being used, the text can also be formatted, such as with a word processing app.

Managing text

To work with text in a document you have created:

The method of moving the cursor is a new feature in iOS 13.

1 To change the insertion point in a document, press on the cursor to pick it up

Moving the cursor.

Hot tip

Once the selection buttons have been accessed, tap once on **Select** to select the previous word, or **Select All** to select all of the text.

2 Drag the cursor to move the insertion point

Moving the cursor.

3 Tap once at the insertion point to access the menu buttons

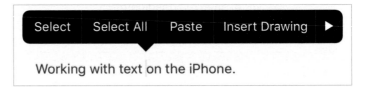

Select   Select All   Paste   Insert Drawing   ▶

Working with text on the iPhone.

Hot tip

The menu buttons in Step 4 can be used to replace the selected word; add bold, italics or underlining to it; or view a definition of it (Look Up), accessed from the button in Step 5. Text menus vary depending on which app is being used.

4 Double-tap on a word to select it. Tap once on one of the menu buttons, as required

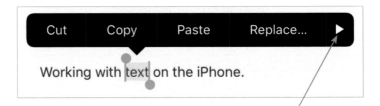

Cut   Copy   Paste   Replace...   ▶

Working with text on the iPhone.

5 Tap once on this button to access more options for working with the selected text (see bottom tip)

Selecting text

Text can be selected using a range of methods:

1 Double-tap on a word to select it

> Once text has been entered with an app on the iPhone it can then be managed. This can involve editing the text. It can also include selecting text.

2 Drag the selection handles to increase, or decrease, the selection. This is a good way to select certain text within a sentence or within a paragraph

> Once text has been entered with an app on the iPhone it can then be managed. This can involve editing the text. It can also include selecting text.

3 Triple-tap on a word to select the whole of its related sentence

> Once text has been entered with an app on the iPhone it can then be managed. This can involve editing the text. It can also include selecting text.

4 Quadruple-tap on a word to select the whole of its related paragraph

> Once text has been entered with an app on the iPhone it can then be managed. This can involve editing the text. It can also include selecting text.

Once text has been selected, there is a range of gestures that can be used to copy and paste it, and also undo the previous action. To copy selected text: pinch inwards over the text with thumb and two fingers. To paste text: swipe outwards with thumb and two fingers, in a dropping motion. To undo the previous action: swipe from right to left with three fingers. These are new features in iOS 13 on the latest iPhone models, and it takes a bit of practice to become proficient in using them.

You can also add someone from your contacts by typing their name into the **To:** field shown in Step 3. As you start typing, names will appear for you to select from. You can type the telephone number of anyone who isn't in your contacts here, too.

When sending messages with the Messages app, you can specify to share your name and photo with the message's recipient. To do this, select **Settings** > **Messages** > **Share Name and Photo** and tap once on the **Choose Name and Photo** button. You can select your current iCloud photo or a Memoji that you have created (see page 96). This is a new feature in iOS 13.

Text Messaging

Text messages sent with the Messages app can either be iMessages or SMS text messages, depending on how they are sent. iMessages are sent using Wi-Fi, to other users with an Apple ID and using an iPhone, iPad, iPod Touch, or a Mac computer. SMS text messages are just sent via your cellular (mobile) carrier. When you send an iMessage, it appears in a blue bubble in the Messages app; when you send a SMS text, it appears in a green bubble.

1   Tap once on the **Messages** app

2   Tap once on this button to create a new message and start a new conversation

3   Tap once on this button to select someone from your contacts

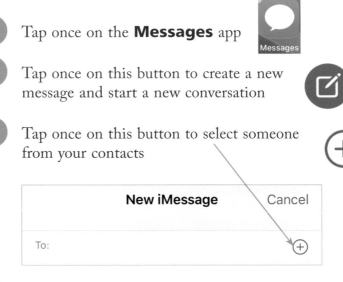

4   Tap once on a contact to select them as the recipient of the new message

5 Tap once here, and type with the keyboard to create a message

Don't forget

When a message has been sent, you are notified underneath it when it has been delivered.

6 Tap once on this button to send a message (it is not available until a message has been composed)

7 As the conversation progresses, each message is displayed in the main window

Hot tip

Press and hold on a message, and tap on the **More...** button that appears. Select a message, or messages, and tap on the **Trash** icon to remove them from the threads. (See pages 101-102 for more information on deleting messages.)

Enhancing Text Messages

Adding emojis

Emojis (small graphical symbols) are very popular in text messages, and there is now a huge range that can be included with iOS 13. To add these:

 Tap once on this button on the keyboard to view the emoji keyboards

 Swipe left and right to view the emoji options. Tap once on an emoji to add it to a message

Emojis can be added automatically from certain words:

 Add text, and tap once on the button in Step 1 above. The items that can be replaced are highlighted

 Tap once on a highlighted word to see the emoji options. Tap once on one to add it to the message

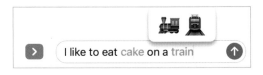

Adding Animojis

Introduced on the iPhone X with iOS 11, the Animoji feature is now available on all new models of iPhone. Animojis are animated stickers that can take on the expressions and voice of the person looking at the iPhone's camera:

Animated Animojis and Memojis require an iPhone X or later, but iOS 13 introduces Animoji and Memoji stickers to older iPhones.

 Create a new message or open an existing conversation

 Tap once on the **Animoji** icon in the App Strip below the text box

Swipe left and right to select the Animoji icon, as required

Tap once on the **Record** button to record a facial expression for the Animoji

Recipients of Animojis should have an iPhone X or later, in order to view them accurately.

Tap once on this button to finish recording

00:18

Tap once on the **Send** button to send the Animoji to the recipient of the message

The expressions for an Animoji can be recorded for up to 30 seconds.

...cont'd

Adding Memojis

An extension of the Animoji feature is the ability to create Memojis in iOS 13 on the latest iPhones. These are customized avatars that can be created to look like yourself. To do this:

The range of items that can be used to customize a Memoji has been updated in iOS 13, including the use of piercings in the Nose category.

Hot tip

For each of the customizable options in Step 4, several different variations can be selected. For instance: for the Skin option, Color and Freckles can be selected; for the Head option, Age and Shape can be selected; and for Facial Hair, there are options for selecting Sideburns and Mustache & Beard color and style.

1. Create a new message or open an existing conversation

2. Tap once on the **Animoji** icon in the App Strip below the text box

3. Swipe to the right and tap once on the **New Memoji** button

New Memoji

4. The Memoji starts as a blank avatar that can be customized. Swipe along the top bar to select options for **Skin**, **Hairstyle**, **Brows**, **Eyes**, **Head**, **Nose**, **Mouth**, **Ears**, **Facial Hair**, **Eyewear**, and **Headwear**

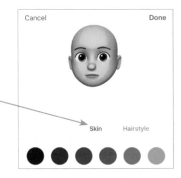

5. Tap once on the **Done** button to complete the Memoji. It is added to the App Strip and can be added to a message by tapping on it here

…cont'd

Full-screen messages
iMessages can also be sent with full-screen effects:

1 Write a message, and press and hold on this button

2 Tap once on the **Screen** button at the top of the window

Send with effect

Bubble   Screen

Screen

3 Different animated options can be selected to accompany the message

4 Swipe to the left, or tap on these buttons to view different animated effects

5 Tap once on this button to send the message (tap once on the cross to delete the animated effect)

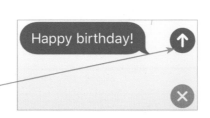

Happy birthday!

Hot tip

With Messages you can show people your location (by sending a map) rather than just telling them. To do this: once a conversation has started, tap once on the person's name at the top of the message window and tap once on the **info** button.

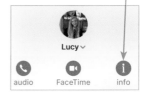

Tap once on **Send My Current Location**, or **Share My Location**.

Send My Current Location

Share My Location

If you select **Share My Location**, this will be updated if your location changes (as long as Location Services is turned On in **Settings** > **Privacy** > **Location Services**).

97

...cont'd

Hot tip

By default, the App Strip button is displayed at the left-hand side of the text box. However, as you start writing a message, this is replaced by the right-pointing arrow in Step 1. Tap once on this to access the App Strip button.

Hot tip

The other Bubble effects in Step 2 are **Slam**, **Loud** and **Gentle**. These determine how the speech bubble appears to the recipient: Slam moves in quickly from left to right; Loud appears initially as a large bubble; Gentle appears initially with small text in the speech bubble. After the initial effects, the bubble returns to its normal size.

Invisible messages

There are several ways to enhance text messages, including sending them in a digital version of invisible ink:

1 Write a message and press and hold on this button

This is a top secret message!

2 Tap once on the **Bubble** button at the top of the window

Bubble

3 Tap once on the **Invisible Ink** button

4 Tap once on this button to send the invisible message

5 The message is sent as a bubble where the content is obscured

6 Swipe on the message to view its content

This is a top secret message!

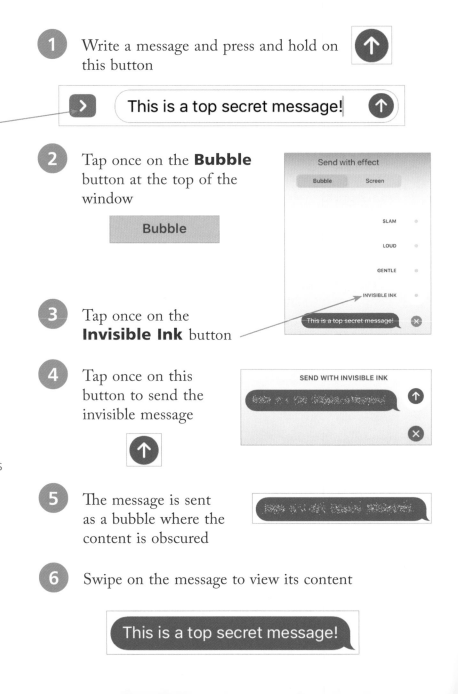

Handwritten messages

To create a more informal message, handwriting can be used.

1 Turn the iPhone into landscape mode, and tap once on this button on the keyboard to access the handwriting panel

2 Write using your finger, or select one of the pre-formatted messages at the bottom of the

panel. Tap once on the **Done** button to add it to a message. The text appears animated to the recipient, as if it is being written on their screen

Quick replies (Tapback)

Instead of writing a full reply to a message it is possible to add a quick reply (also known as Tapback), which consists of an appropriate icon that is attached to the original message:

1 Press and hold on the message to which you want to add a quick reply, and tap once on one of the icons

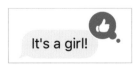

2 The selected icon is added to the original message, and this is displayed to the sender of the message

It's a girl!

Hot tip

You can also send family and friends audio clips in an iMessage so that they can hear from you too. To do this, press and hold on the microphone icon at the right-hand side of the text box, and record your message (see next page).

Don't forget

Money can be transferred to other people by tapping on this button on the App Strip. To use this service, Apple Pay and Apple Pay Cash have to be set up on your own iPhone and the recipient's. At the time of printing, this service is only available in the US.

Voice Typing

On the keyboard there is also a voice-typing option, which enables you to enter text by speaking into a microphone, rather than typing on the keyboard. This is On by default.

Using voice typing

Voice typing (dictation) can be used with any app with a text input function. To do this:

Beware

Voice typing is not an exact science, and you may find that some strange examples appear. The best results are created if you speak as clearly as possible and reasonably slowly.

Hot tip

Dictation can be turned **On** or **Off** in **Settings** > **General** > **Keyboard** > **Enable Dictation**.

Don't forget

There are other voice-typing apps available from the App Store. One to try is Dragon Anywhere.

1 Press and hold on this button on the keyboard to activate the voice-typing microphone. Speak into the microphone to record text

2 As the voice-typing function is processing the recording, this screen appears

3 Tap once on this button to finish recording and return to the standard keyboard

4 Once the recording has been processed, the text appears in the app

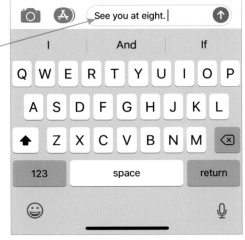

Managing Messages

Text conversations with individuals can become quite lengthy so it is sometimes a good idea to remove some messages, while still keeping the conversation going.

1 As a conversation with one person progresses, it moves downwards in the window

You can copy a message by tapping once on the **Copy** button in Step 2 and then pasting it into another app, such as an email. To do this, press and hold on an open email, and tap once on the **Paste** button.

2 Press and hold on a message that you want to delete, and tap once on the **More...** button (pressing and holding on a message also activates the Tapback option; see page 99)

3 Tap once next to any message that you want to delete, so that a white tick in a blue circle appears

Settings for the Messages app can be applied in the Settings app. These include: **Send Read Receipts**, to indicate that you have read the message sent; and **Send as SMS**, to send a SMS message when iMessage is unavailable.

4 Tap once on the Trash icon to delete the selected message(s)

...cont'd

Whole conversations can also be deleted:

1 From a conversation, tap once on the **Back** button to view all of your conversations

2 Tap once on the **Edit** button

Don't forget

It is good housekeeping to delete conversations that have finished, otherwise you may end up with a long list of different ones.

3 Tap once next to any whole conversation(s) that you want to delete

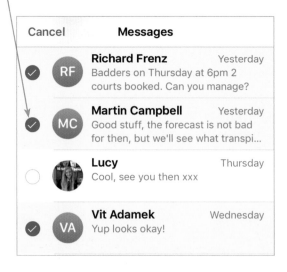

4 Tap once on the **Delete** button at the bottom right-hand corner of the screen to remove the selected conversation(s)

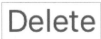

6 Camera and Photos

The iPhone has a high-quality camera, and the Photos app for viewing your photos.

To take a quick photo, open the **Camera** app and press on either of the Volume buttons on the side of the iPhone.

If the Ultra Wide option is used on the iPhone 11 models, an area up to four times greater than the Telephoto view can be included in a photo. This is an excellent option when capturing landscape photos in particular. This is a new feature on the iPhone 11 Pro and 11 Pro Max using iOS 13.

The iPhone Camera

The cameras on the iPhone 11 range are the most revolutionary to be included with any iPhone, and they take the art of digital photography on a smartphone to a new level. The iPhone 11 Pro and Pro Max are particularly ground-breaking for iPhones as they include three separate lenses, to enable a far greater area to be included in photos.

iPhone 11 camera
The main iPhone 11 camera consists of two lenses:

Wide

Ultra Wide

Tap on these buttons to switch between the two lenses.

iPhone 11 Pro and Pro Max camera
The camera on the iPhone 11 Pro and Pro Max consists of three lenses:

Wide

Ultra Wide

Telephoto

Tap on the same buttons as above for the iPhone 11 (the Pro and Pro Max both have an extra button that corresponds with the additional lens) to switch between the three lenses, or

drag on the dial to change the angle of view.

Camera functionality

The general functionality of the iPhone 11 cameras can be accessed within the Camera app:

1 Tap once on the **Camera** app

2 Swipe here and select the **Photo** option. Tap once on this button to capture a photo

3 Tap once on this button to swap between the front or back cameras on the iPhone

Swipe left or right just above the shutter button, to access the different shooting options:

1 Tap once on the **Square** button to capture photos at this ratio

2 Tap once on the **Video** button and press the red shutter button to take a video

3 Tap once on the **Time-Lapse** button and press the shutter button (which appears in red with a ring around it) to create a time-lapse image: the camera keeps taking photos periodically until you press the shutter button again

Videos can also be captured from the Photo option. To do this, press and hold on the shutter button until it turns into the video button. The video should start recording automatically. This is a new feature in iOS 13 on all of the iPhone 11 models. Tap once on this button to end a video capture. When any video is captured it is stored within the **Photos** app.

Use the front-facing TrueDepth camera to take selfies (self-portraits of yourself, or a group of people). Use the video button to take a slow-motion video selfie, which Apple has decided to call a "slowfie". This is a new feature with the iPhone 11 range and iOS 13.

...cont'd

4 Tap once on the **Slo-Mo** button and press the red shutter button to take a slow-motion video

5 Tap once on the **Pano** button to create a panoramic image

6 Move the iPhone slowly to the right to create the panorama. Each photo will be taken automatically when the camera is in the correct position

7 Tap once on the **Portrait** button to access options for portrait shots (see next page)

Camera functions

The buttons at the top of the camera window can be used to create additional functionality.

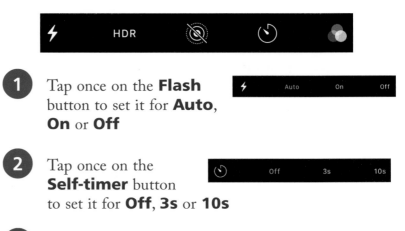

1 Tap once on the **Flash** button to set it for **Auto**, **On** or **Off**

2 Tap once on the **Self-timer** button to set it for **Off**, **3s** or **10s**

3 Tap once on the **HDR** button so it does not have a line through it to take a composite photo of three separate images, to achieve the best exposure

Portrait mode

Taking photos of people is one of the most common uses for the iPhone's camera. Using the iPhone camera in Portrait mode, it is possible to change the lighting of the photo. To do this:

1 Select the **Portrait** option as shown on the previous page

2 The lighting options are shown above the **Portrait** button. Tap once on each option to select the required lighting mode

Adding depth of field

Portrait photos can be enhanced by blurring the background behind the subject, so that they are more prominent. This is known as "depth of field". To do this:

1 Open the **Photos** app and tap once on a photo taken in Portrait mode

2 Tap once on the **f** number icon in the top left-hand corner, and drag this slider to apply a blurred effect to the background of the photo. The main subject will remain unchanged

3 Tap once of the **Done** button to apply the depth-of-field effect to the photo

Photo Settings

iCloud sharing

Certain photo options can be applied within Settings. Several of these are to do with storing and sharing your photos via iCloud. To access these:

 Tap once on the **Settings** app

 Tap once on the **Photos** tab

 Drag the **iCloud Photos** button **On** to upload your whole iPhone photo library to the iCloud. You will then be able to access this from any other Apple devices that you have. Similarly, photos on your other Apple devices can also be uploaded to the iCloud, and these will be available on your iPhone

iCloud Photos	⬤

 Drag the **Upload to My Photo Stream** button **On** to enable all new photos and videos from your iPhone to be uploaded automatically to iCloud

Upload to My Photo Stream	⬤

5 Drag the **Shared Albums** button **On** to allow you to create albums within the Photos app that can then be shared with other people via iCloud

Shared Albums	⬤

Drag the **Grid** button in the **Camera** settings **On** to place a grid over the screen when you are taking photos with the camera, if required. This can be used to help compose photos by placing subjects using the grid.

Viewing Photos

Once photos have been captured, they can be viewed and organized in the Photos app. To do this:

1   Tap once on the **Photos** app

2   Tap once on the **Photos** button on the bottom toolbar to view photos according to when they were taken, by **Years**, **Months**, **Days**, or **All Photos**

3   Photos are displayed according to the category selected in Step 2

4   If photos are displayed in **Days** or **All Photos** mode, tap once on the **Select** button to select specific photos by tapping on them, or by dragging over several photos

5   Once photos have been selected, or if they are being viewed at full size, tap once on this button to **Share** them

The Photos app has been updated on the iPhone with iOS 13.

Hot tip

Double-tap with one finger on a full-size photo to zoom in on it. Double-tap again to zoom back out. To zoom in to a greater degree, swipe outwards with thumb and forefinger. To zoom back out, pinch inwards with thumb and forefinger.

Hot tip

Tap once on the **Albums** button on the bottom toolbar to view available albums for storing photos. Tap once on this button to create a new album and select items to go in it.

For You Tab

In the Photos app, the For You section is where the best of your photos are selected and displayed automatically. To use this:

1 Tap once on the **For You** button on the bottom toolbar of the Photos app

2 Memories are displayed in the **For You** section. These are collections of photos created by the Photos app, using what it determines are the best shots for a related series of photos

3 Tap once on a Memory to view its details. Tap once on the **Play** button to view a full-screen slideshow of all of the images, including music

4 Swipe down the For You page to access more options for how photos are grouped and organized

Hot tip

When a Memory is playing as shown in Step 3, tap once on an image on the screen and tap once on the **Edit** button in the top right-hand corner to access the editing options for the Memory. These include editing the music, title, duration, and the items in the Memory. Tap once on the **Done** button in the bottom right-hand corner to exit the editing mode.

Editing Photos

The Photos app has options to perform a range of photo-editing operations. To use these:

 Open a photo at full-screen size and tap once on the **Edit** button to access the editing tools, on the bottom toolbar

Edit

Cancel · · Done

 Tap once on the **Adjust** button to access color-editing options

 Tap once on the **Auto** button to have auto-coloring editing applied to the photo

 Swipe from right to left to access the full range of the Adjust options

EXPOSURE

 For each option, drag the slider to apply the required level of the effect

BRILLIANCE

The range of editing options has been updated in iOS 13.

Beware

Editing changes are made to the original photo once the changes have been saved. These will also apply to any albums into which the photo has been placed.

Don't forget

The Adjust color-editing options include: Exposure; Brilliance; Highlights; Shadows; Contrast; Brightness; Saturation; and Vibrance.

Videos can now also have the same range of editing effects applied to them as still photos. This is a new feature in iOS 13.

...cont'd

 Tap once on the **Filters** button in Step 1 on page 111 to select special effects to be applied to the photo. Swipe left and right here to view the available filters. Tap once on one to apply it

Hot tip

If you reopen a photo that has been edited and closed, you have an option to **Revert** to its original state, before it was edited.

 Tap once on the **Auto** button in Step 1 on page 111 to access options for rotating the photo and cropping it, by dragging the resizing handles around the border of the photo. Use these options to, from left to right: straighten the photo by dragging the slider; flip it vertically; and flip it horizontally

 For each function, tap once on the **Done** button to save the photo with the selected changes

 Tap once on the **Cancel** button to quit the editing process

7 The Online World

This chapter shows how to use your iPhone to keep ahead in the fast-moving world of online communications: using the Safari app to access content on the web; email; social media; and video calls.

Getting Online

Connecting to Wi-Fi is one of the main ways that the iPhone can get online access. You will need to have an Internet Service Provider and a Wi-Fi router to connect to the internet. Once this is in place, you will be able to connect to a Wi-Fi network:

You can also get online access through your cellular network, which is provided by your phone network supplier. However, data charges may apply for this.

1 Tap once on the **Settings** app

Settings

2 Tap once on the **Wi-Fi** tab

📶 Wi-Fi   Not Connected ›

3 Ensure the **Wi-Fi** button is in the **On** position

‹ Settings   **Wi-Fi**

Wi-Fi ⬤

NETWORKS

PLUSNET-TXJ5   🔒 📶 ⓘ

Virgin Media   🔒 📶 ⓘ

VM2311170   🔒 📶 ⓘ

4 Available networks are shown here. Tap once on one to select it

If you are connecting to your home Wi-Fi network, the iPhone should connect automatically each time, after it has been set up. If you are connecting in a public Wi-Fi area, you will be asked which network you would like to join.

5 Enter a password for your Wi-Fi router

Enter the password for "PlusnetWireless792287"

Cancel   **Enter Password**   Join

Password   •••••••••

6 Tap once on the **Join** button   Join

7 Once a network has been joined, a tick appears next to it. This now provides access to the internet

‹ Settings   **Wi-Fi**

Wi-Fi ⬤

✓ PlusnetWireless792287   🔒 📶 ⓘ

Safari Settings

Safari is the default web browser on the iPhone, and it can be used to bring the web to your iPhone. Before you start using Safari, there are a range of settings that can be applied:

 1 Tap once on the **Settings** app

2 Tap once on the **Safari** tab

3 Make selections under the **Search** section for the default search engine, options for suggestions appearing as you type search words and phrases, and preloading the top-rating page in a search

4 Make selections under the **General** section for entering passwords, specifying the items for the Favorites window, and blocking pop-ups

5 Make selections under the **Privacy & Security** section for blocking cookies, warning about fraudulent websites, checking to see whether websites accept Apple Pay, and clearing your web browsing history and web data

Because of the proliferation of apps available for the iPhone, you may find that you use Safari less than on a desktop or laptop computer. For example, most major news outlets have their own apps that can be used as stand-alone items, rather than having to use Safari to access the site. Look for apps for your favorite websites in the App Store, as a shortcut for accessing them quickly.

The latest iPhones have a setting for **Show Tab Bar**, which displays the open tabs along the top of the Safari window, if the iPhone is being used in landscape mode.

Web Browsing with Safari

To start browsing the web with Safari and enjoy the variety of the information within it:

The Safari Start page has been updated in iOS 13, with the inclusion of Siri suggestions.

1 Tap once on the **Safari** app

2 Enter a website address here in the Address Bar, or tap once on one of the items in the Start page – e.g. one of the Favorites, or one of the Siri suggestions

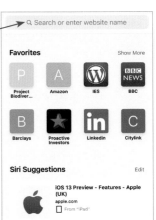

3 As you type in the Address Bar, website suggestions appear, and also search suggestions with Google

4 When you access a web page, use these buttons to visit the next and previous pages

The **Share** button in Step 5 can be used to share a web page via Message, Mail, or social media sites such as Facebook or Twitter. It can also be used to add a web page link to a Note.

5 Use this button to share a web page

6 Use this button to view bookmarks

7 Use this button to view, add and delete tabs (see pages 118-119)

Adding bookmarks

Everyone has favorite websites that they visit, and in Safari it is possible to mark these with bookmarks so that they can be accessed quickly. To do this:

1 Tap once on this button on the bottom toolbar

2 Tap once on the **Add Bookmark** button

Add Bookmark

3 Select a name and location for the bookmark, and tap once on the **Save** button

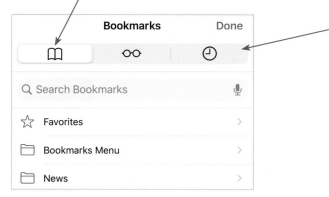

Cancel	**Add Bookmark**	Save

Edinburgh Zoo Live Panda cam | Edinl ⊗

http://www.edinburghzoo.org.uk/webca...

LOCATION

☆ Favorites

4 Tap once on the **Bookmarks** button, and tap once here to view your bookmarks

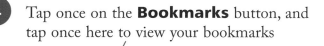

	Bookmarks	Done

🔖 ∞ 🕐

🔍 Search Bookmarks 🎤

☆ Favorites >

📁 Bookmarks Menu >

📁 News >

Hot tip

If the bottom toolbar is not visible on a web page, swipe downwards on the page to view it.

Don't forget

The **Bookmarks** button in Step 4 can also be used to access any Reading List items that have been stored. These are added from the **Share** button in Step 1, and enable items to be saved and read later, even if you are not connected to the internet. (The third button in Step 4 is for accessing your web browsing history.)

Reading List

🔖 ∞ 🕐

In Easy Steps Smart Learning with In Easy Steps books
ineasysteps.com

Top Smart Home Entertainment Devices for 2019 | For the Smart Home
forthesmarthome.com
Our guide to the top smart home entertainment devices brings the latest...

Using Tabs in Safari

In keeping with most modern web browsers, Safari uses tabs so that you can have several websites open at the same time. However, due to the fact that a smartphone's screen is smaller than those on a desktop or laptop computer, tabs operate in a specific way on the iPhone. To use tabs:

Hot tip

Press and hold on a tab to drag it into a different position in Tab View.

Press and hold the Tab button to get the option to close all open tabs in one go.

Don't forget

Tap once on the **Done** button at the bottom of the Tab View window to exit this and return to the web page that was being viewed when Tab View was activated.

1 Open Safari and open a website. Tap once on this button on the bottom toolbar to view all currently-open tabs

2 Swipe up and down in Tab View to view all of the open tabs. Tap once on one to view that web page at full size

3 Swipe to the bottom of the page to view any tabs that you have open on any other Apple devices, such as an iPad

Opening tabs

To open more tabs in Safari on your iPhone:

1 Open the Tab View window as shown opposite, and tap once on this button

2 Open the new tab by entering a web address in the Address Bar, or by tapping once on one of the items in the Favorites window

Hot tip

The items that appear in the Favorites window can be specified with the Safari settings: **Settings** > **Safari** > **Favorites** and by then selecting a category. This page will appear when a new tab is opened, and also when you tap in the Address Bar to enter a web address.

3 Tap once on the **Private** button in Tab View to open a new tab that is not recorded in your web history

Private

4 Open the private tab in the same way as a regular one. This is indicated by a dark bar at the top of the window

5 Tap once on this button to close any tab in Tab View

The range of web page options is a new feature in iOS 13.

In Reader View, the button in the Address Bar turns black. Tap once on it to access options for how Reader View is displayed, including text size, background color and font. It can also be used to hide the Reader View and return to the full web page.

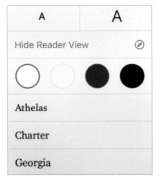

Web Page Options

Being able to view web pages in the way that you want is an important part of any browsing experience, and Safari offers various options for displaying web pages. These can be accessed from the left-hand side of the Address Bar:

1 Tap once on this button in the Address Bar **AA**

2 The web page options are displayed

3 Tap once on these buttons to change the text size of a web page

4 Tap once on the **Show Reader View** button to view the current web page with just text and no extra content, such as images

Show Reader View

5 Tap once on the **Hide Toolbar** button to hide the toolbar and create a larger viewing area for the current web page

Hide Toolbar

6 Tap once on the **Request Mobile Website** button to view a mobile version of the website, if there is one

Request Mobile Website

7 Tap once on the **Website Settings** button to access settings for the website being viewed

Website Settings

Download Manager

Web pages are a very sophisticated way of conveying information in a variety of different formats, not just the initial page that you see. One way of doing this is to present items that can be downloaded and then viewed in a web browser or a different app, depending on the format of the information. These are links to separate files, not just links to another web page. Some file formats for downloading documents include word processing formats, PDF files, and photo formats. Within Safari there is an option for managing items that have been downloaded, and they can also be stored within the Files app. To use this:

1. Find a file to download in Safari

2. Press and hold on the link to the file and tap once on the **Download Linked File** option

3. Tap once on the **Download Manager** button on the top toolbar to view items that have been downloaded and the progress of any current downloads. Tap once on the **Clear** button to hide the window and the Download button (the downloaded file will still be available in the Files app – see next Step)

4. Open the **Files** app

5. Tap once on the **Downloads** folder and tap once on items within it to open them

The Download Manager is a new feature in iOS 13.

Hot tip

Since downloads are stored in the Files app they can be accessed at any time, not just when Safari is open.

Hot tip

The folder into which downloads are stored can be specified in **Settings** > **Safari** > **Downloads**, and then select a location.

Don't forget

When files are opened from the Files app they are done so in a compatible app – e.g. a Word document will be opened in a word processing app, and a music file in a music app, rather than in Safari.

Setting up an Email Account

Email accounts
Email settings can be specified within the Settings app.
Different email accounts can also be added there.

1 Tap once on the **Settings** app

2 Tap once on the **Passwords & Accounts** tab

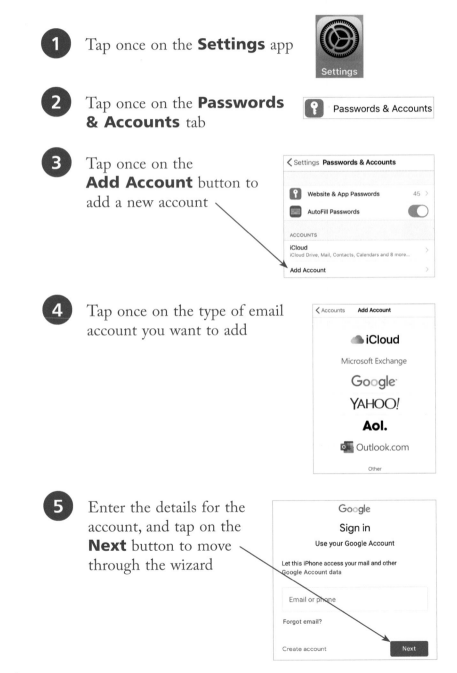

3 Tap once on the **Add Account** button to add a new account

4 Tap once on the type of email account you want to add

Hot tip

If your email provider is not on the **Add Account** list, tap once on **Other** at the bottom of the list and complete the account details using the information from your email provider.

5 Enter the details for the account, and tap on the **Next** button to move through the wizard

6 Drag these buttons **On** or **Off** to specify which functions are to be available for the required account. Tap once on the **Save** button

7 Each new account is added under the **Accounts** heading of the Mail section

If you set up more than one email account, messages from all of them can be downloaded and displayed by **Mail**.

Email settings

Email settings can be specified within the Settings app:

1 Under the **Mail** section there are several options for how Mail operates and looks. These include how much of an email will be previewed in your Inbox, and options for accessing actions by swiping on an email

The **Organize by Thread** option can be turned **On** to show connected email conversations within your Inbox. If there is a thread of emails, this is indicated by this symbol.

Monday >

Tap on it once to view the thread.

Emailing

Email on the iPhone is created, sent and received using the Mail app (although other email apps can be downloaded from the App Store). This provides a range of functionality for managing emails and responding to them.

Accessing Mail

To access Mail and start sending and receiving emails:

1 Tap once on the **Mail** app (the red icon in the corner displays the number of unread emails in your Inbox)

2 Tap once on a message to display it in the main panel

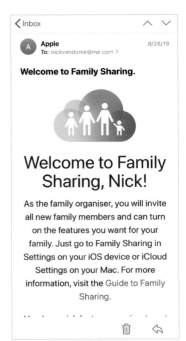

3 Use these buttons to, from left to right: delete a message; or respond to a message (see next page)

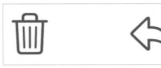

4 Tap once on this button to reply to a message, reply to everyone in a conversation, forward it to a new recipient, delete it, flag it, mark it as unread, or move it to a folder

The Reply menu has been updated with a greater range of options in iOS 13.

Hot tip

If the recipient is included in your Contacts app, their details will appear as you type in Step 2. Tap once on a name to add it in the To: box.

Creating email

To create and send an email:

1 Tap once on this button to create a new message

2 Enter a recipient name in the **To:** box

When writing an email, these buttons above the keyboard can be used to add content to the email, from left to right: change the text size; add a photo; take a photo; add a document; scan a document; or add a freehand sketch. This is a new feature in iOS 13.

3 Enter a subject and body text

4 Tap once on the **Send** button to send the email to the recipient

Having a Video Chat

Video chatting is a very personal and interactive way to keep in touch with family and friends around the world. The FaceTime app provides this facility with other iPhone, iPad, iPod Touch and Mac computer users with FaceTime. To use FaceTime for video chatting:

Don't forget

To make video calls with FaceTime you need an active internet connection and to be signed in with your Apple ID.

Hot tip

The contacts for FaceTime calls are taken from the iPhone Contacts app. You can also add new contacts directly to the contacts list by tapping once on the **+** sign and adding the relevant details for the new contact.

Don't forget

Skype is another option for making free video calls to other Skype users. The app can be downloaded from the App Store.

1 Tap once on the **FaceTime** app

2 Tap once on this button to start a new video chat and tap once here to select a contact

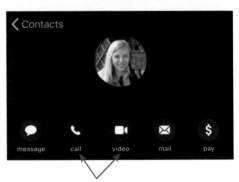

3 Tap once on a contact to access their details for making a FaceTime call

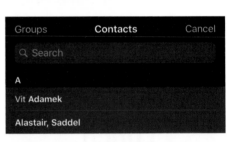

4 Tap once on their phone number or email address to make a FaceTime call. The recipient must have FaceTime on their iPhone, iPad, iPod Touch or Mac computer. Tap once on these buttons to make a video or audio call

5 Once you have selected a contact, FaceTime starts

connecting to them and displays this at the top of the screen

6 When you have connected, your contact appears in the main window and you appear in a picture-in-picture thumbnail in the corner

7 Tap once on this button to access effects options that can be added to your own video display, including filters and text

Tap once on the **effects** button in Step 7 and tap once on this button to access any Animojis or Memojis that you have created (see pages 95-96). Tap once on one to superimpose it over your own face in the FaceTime window. (iPhone X models and later only).

8 Tap once on these buttons to access additional options: muting the conversation and flipping the camera view

9 Tap once on this button to end a FaceTime call

Adding Social Media

Using social media sites such as Facebook, Twitter, and Snapchat to keep in touch with family and friends has now become common across all generations. On the iPhone with iOS 13, it is possible to link to these accounts so that you can share content to them from your iPhone, and also view updates through the Notification Center. To add social media apps to your iPhone:

Hot tip

Updates can be set to appear in your **Notification Center**. Open **Settings**, and tap once on the **Notifications** tab. Under the **Notification Style** heading, tap once on the social media site and select options for how you would like the notifications to appear.

1 Open the App Store and navigate to the **Apps > Categories > Social Networking** section

2 Tap once on the required apps to download them to your iPhone

3 Tap once on an app to open it

Don't forget

Social media sites can be accessed from their own apps on the iPhone, and also from their respective websites, using Safari.

4 If you already have an account with the social media service, enter your login details, or tap once on the **Create New Account** button to create a new account

8 Hands on with Apps

Apps are the items that give the iPhone its functionality. This chapter details the built-in apps, and also shows how to access those in the App Store.

What is an App?

An app is just a more modern name for a computer program. Initially, it was used in relation to mobile devices such as the iPhone and the iPad, but it is now becoming more widely used with desktop and laptop computers, for both Mac and Windows operating systems.

On the iPhone there are two types of apps:

You need an active internet connection to download apps from the App Store.

- **Built-in apps**. These are the apps that come already installed on the iPhone.

- **App Store apps**. These are apps that can be downloaded from the online App Store. There is a huge range of apps available there, covering a variety of different categories. Some are free, while others have to be paid for. The apps in the App Store are updated and added to on a daily basis, so there are always new ones to explore.

Within a number of apps there is a **Share** button that can be used to share items through a variety of methods, including iMessages, email, Facebook and Twitter.

There are also two important points about apps (both built-in and those from the App Store) to remember:

- Apart from some of the built-in apps, the majority of apps do not interact with each other. This means that there is less chance of viruses being transmitted from app to app on your iPhone, and they can operate without a reliance on other apps.

- Content created by apps is saved within the app itself, rather than within a file structure on your iPhone; e.g. if you create a note in the Notes app, it is saved there; if you take a photo, it is saved in the Photos app. Content is usually also saved automatically when it is created or edited, so you do not have to worry about saving it as you work on it.

Built-in Apps

The built-in iPhone apps are the ones that appear on the Home screen when you first get your iPhone:

- **App Store**. This can be used to access the online App Store, from where additional apps can be downloaded and updated.

- **Books**. This is an app for downloading electronic books, which can then be read on the iPhone.

- **Calculator**. This is a basic calculator, which can also be accessed from the Control Center.

- **Calendar**. An app for storing appointments, important dates, and other calendar information. It can be synced with iCloud.

- **Camera**. This gives direct access to the front-facing and rear-facing iPhone cameras.

- **Clock**. This displays the current time, and can be used to view the time in different countries. It also has an alarm clock and a stopwatch.

- **Compass**. This can be used to show you the direction of North. You can give the compass access to your location so that you can follow it from where you are.

- **Contacts**. An address book app. Once contacts are added here they can then also be accessed from other apps, such as Mail.

- **FaceTime**. This app uses the front-facing FaceTime camera to hold video or audio chats with compatible Apple devices.

- **Files**. This is used to back up items and make them available to other Apple devices.

NEW

When you first open an app it will display options for location access; e.g. whether the app can access your current location. The options are for: allowing access while using the app; allowing access once; or not allowing access. If you select to allow access once, you will be prompted with the same query the next time you use the app. This is a new feature in iOS 13, designed to prevent apps from constantly having access to your location. Location settings can also be applied in **Settings** > **Privacy** > **Location Services** and then tap once on the app name.

Hot tip

If you don't want your contacts to be accessed by other apps, open **Settings** > **Privacy** > **Contacts** and drag the button for these apps to **Off**.

...cont'd

Although iTunes has been removed from Mac computers with the macOS operating system, the iTunes Store is still a part of iOS 13 and can be used to download a range of content, including music and movies. These items are then displayed in their respective apps; i.e. the Music and TV apps.

You need an Apple ID to obtain content from the iTunes Store and Books.

- **Find My**. This can be used to view the location of family and friends, based on their Apple mobile devices and Mac computers. See pages 184-185.

- **Health**. This stores and collates a range of health information. See pages 145-147.

- **Home**. This is a new app in iOS 13 that can be used to control certain compatible functions within the home, such as heating controls.

- **iTunes Store**. This app can be used to browse the iTunes Store, where content can be downloaded to your iPhone.

- **Mail**. This is the email app for sending and receiving email on your iPhone.

- **Maps**. Use this app to view maps from around the world, find specific locations, and get directions to destinations.

- **Measure**. This can be used to measure the length or perimeter of items.

- **Messages**. This is the iPhone messaging service, which can be used for SMS text messages and iMessages between compatible Apple devices.

- **Music**. An app for playing music on your iPhone and also viewing cover artwork. You can also use it to create your own playlists.

- **News**. This collates news stories from numerous online publications and categories.

- **Notes**. If you need to jot down your thoughts or ideas, this app is perfect for just that.

- **Photos**. This is an app for viewing and editing your photos and videos, and creating slideshows. It can also be used to share photos.

- **Podcasts**. This can be used to download podcasts from within the App Store.

- **Reminders**. Use this app to help keep organized, when you want to create to-do lists and set reminders for events.

- **Safari**. The Apple web browser that has been developed for viewing the web on your iPhone.

- **Settings**. This contains a range of settings for the iPhone (see pages 20-21 for details).

- **Stocks**. Use this to display the latest stock market prices and add your own companies.

- **Tips**. This can be used to display tips and hints for items on your iPhone.

- **TV**. This is an app for viewing videos from the TV Store, and also streaming them to a larger HDTV monitor.

- **Voice Memos**. This can be used to record short audio reminders that can be stored and played on the iPhone.

- **Wallet**. This can be used to store credit, debit, and storecard details, for making payments with Apple Pay (in some locations).

- **Watch**. This can be used to pair an iPhone with the Apple Watch and apply a range of settings.

- **Weather**. Displays weather details for your location and destinations around the world.

Podcasts are audio or video programs, and they cover an extensive range of subjects.

Some of the default apps are located on the second Home screen, or within the **Extras** folder.

The TV app can also be used to access the Apple TV+ service. This is a subscription service for streaming original TV shows and movies from Apple TV. There is a 7-day free trial and then the service costs $5.99 a month in the US and £4.99 in the UK.

About the App Store

While the built-in apps that come with the iPhone are flexible and versatile, apps really come into their own when you connect to the App Store. This is an online resource, and there are thousands of apps there that can be downloaded and then used on your iPhone, including categories from Lifestyle to Medical and Travel.

To use the App Store, you must first have an Apple ID. This can be obtained when you first connect to the App Store. Once you have an Apple ID, you can start exploring the App Store and the apps within it:

The items within the Today section of the App Store change on a regular basis, so it is always worth looking at it from time to time.

 Tap once on the **App Store** app on the Home screen

 The latest available apps are displayed on the Homepage of the App Store, including the featured and best new apps

Tap on these buttons to view items according to **Today**, **Games**, **Apps**, **Arcade** and **Updates**

Viewing apps

To view apps in the App Store and read about their content and functionality:

1 Tap once on an app

2 General details about the app are displayed

3 Swipe left or right here to view additional information about the app, and view details

If it is an upgraded version of an app, this page will include details of any fixes and improvements that have been made.

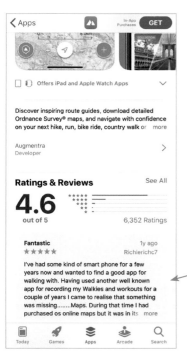

4 Scroll down the page to see additional information including reviews and new items in this version of the app

Finding Apps

Featured

Within the App Store, apps are separated into categories according to type. This enables you to find apps according to particular subjects. To do this:

Don't forget

Some apps will differ depending on the geographical location from which you are accessing the App Store.

Hot tip

There are an increasing number of AR (Augmented Reality) apps in the App Store. These are apps that combine real-life images, either within the app or from the device's camera, that are used with graphical elements; e.g. constellations can be drawn over an image of the sky in an astronomy app.

1 Tap once on the **Apps** button on the toolbar at the bottom of the App Store

2 Scroll up and down to view all of the sections within the Apps Homepage, and scroll left and right to view items within each section heading

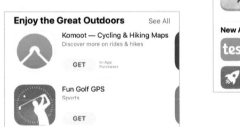

3 Scroll down the page to the **Top Categories** section, and tap once on the **See All** button to view the full range of categories of apps

Top Categories	See All
AR Apps	
Photo & Video	
Entertainment	
Health & Fitness	
Lifestyle	
Travel	

4 Tap once on a category to view the items within it. This can be navigated in the same way as the main Homepage in the App Store; e.g. swipe up and down to view sections, and left and right on each panel to view the available apps

Top Charts
To find the top-rated apps:

1 Tap once on the **Apps** button on the toolbar at the bottom of the App Store

2 Scroll down the page to view the **Top Paid** and **Top Free** apps

3 Tap once on the **See All** button to view all of the Top Paid or Top Charts apps

Searching for apps
Another way to find apps is with the App Store Search box, which appears at the top of the App Store window once it has been accessed. To use this to find apps:

1 Tap once on the **Search** button at the bottom of the window to access the Search box

2 Tap in the Search box to activate the keyboard and enter a search keyword or phrase

3 Suggested apps appear as you are typing

4 Tap on an app to view it

Hot tip

Do not limit yourself to just viewing the top apps. Although these are the most popular, there are also a lot of excellent apps within each category.

Don't forget

For more information about using the iPhone virtual keyboard, see pages 82-91.

Downloading Apps

When you identify an app that you would like to use, it can be downloaded to your iPhone. To do this:

Apps usually download in a few minutes or less, depending on the speed of your Wi-Fi connection.

Some apps have "in-app purchases". This is additional content that has to be paid for when it is downloaded.

1 Find the app you want, using the **App Store**

2 Tap once on the **Price** or **Get** button

3 If Face ID is used on the phone, double-click the side button. (For iPhones with a Home button, press on the Home button with the finger that was used to set up Touch ID)

4 The app is downloaded to the next available space on the Home screen

Updating Apps

The publishers of apps provide updates that bring new features and improvements. You do not have to check your apps to see if there are updates – you can set them to be updated automatically through the Settings app. To do this:

1. Open **Settings** and tap on the **iTunes & App Store** tab

You should keep your apps as up-to-date as possible to take advantage of software fixes and any updates to the iPhone operating system (iOS).

2. Drag the **App Updates** button under **Automatic Downloads On** to enable automatic updates for apps

Managing your Apps

As more apps are added it can become hard to find the ones you want, particularly if you have to swipe between several screens. However, it is possible to organize apps into individual folders to make using them more manageable. To do this:

1 Press on an app until it starts to jiggle and a cross appears at the top-left corner. (The cross can be used to delete the app – see next page)

2 Drag the app over another one

3 A folder is created, containing the two apps. The folder is given a default name, usually based on the category of the first app

4 Tap once on the folder name and type a new name, if required

5 Tap on the **done** button on the keyboard to finish creating the folder

6 The folder is added on the Home screen. Tap on this to access the items within it (press and hold on it to move it)

Deleting Apps

If you decide that you do not want certain apps anymore, they can be deleted from your iPhone. However, they remain in the iCloud so that you can reinstall them if you change your mind. This also means that if you delete an app by mistake, you can get it back from the App Store without having to pay for it again. To do this:

 Press on an app until it starts to jiggle and a cross appears at the top-left corner

 Tap once on the cross to delete the app. In the Delete dialog box, tap once on the **Delete** button

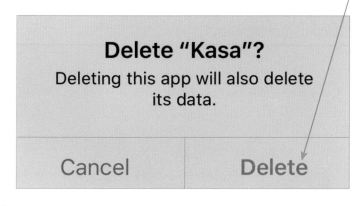

Delete "Kasa"?
Deleting this app will also delete its data.

| Cancel | Delete |

 To reinstall a deleted app, tap once on the **App Store** app

App Store

 Tap once on the **Account** icon at the top of the window

Beware

If you delete an app it will also delete any data that has been compiled with that app, even if you reinstall it from the App Store.

Don't forget

When you long press on an app, a menu appears on the screen. If you keep pressing, the menu disappears and the icon in Step 1 becomes available.

Hot tip

Most of the built-in apps can now be deleted in iOS 13. The ones that cannot be deleted are: App Store, Camera, Clock, Find My, Health, Messages, Phone, Photos, Safari, Settings, and Wallet.

...cont'd

5 Tap once on the **Purchased** button

Nick Vandome nickvandome@mac.com	>
Purchased	>

6 Tap once on the **My Purchases** button

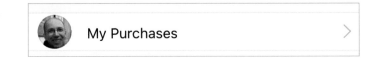

My Purchases	>

Don't
forget

All of the apps that
you have downloaded,
including those on
other Apple devices,
will be listed in the
My Purchases
section of the App
Store.

7 Tap once on the **iCloud** button next to
an app that has been installed and then
deleted, to reinstall it

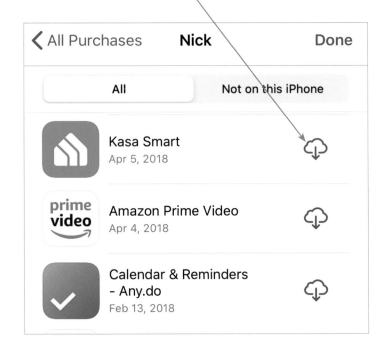

< All Purchases   **Nick**   Done

All	Not on this iPhone

	Kasa Smart Apr 5, 2018	⬇
prime video	Amazon Prime Video Apr 4, 2018	⬇
✓	Calendar & Reminders - Any.do Feb 13, 2018	⬇

9 Apps for Every Day

The iPhone has apps to make your day-to-day life run more smoothly, including staying healthy, keeping notes, and reading the news.

Apple Watch with the iPhone

Working with the Apple Watch

In April 2015 Apple introduced the Apple Watch, and it has now reached its fifth version: Apple Watch Series 5. This is much more than a watch, though: it is also a body monitoring device. It has a number of sensors on the back,

which monitor information such as heart rate and body movement. There is also an activity app to measure your fitness activities. A lot of this data can be sent to the Health app on the iPhone, where it can be stored and analyzed in greater depth.

The Apple Watch Series 5 has an always-on display (the previous versions only showed the display when the watch on the wearer's wrist was moved towards their face), and battery life of up to 18 hours.

Previous versions of the Apple Watch had to be paired (linked) with the iPhone to access certain functionality, such as making and receiving calls. However, the Apple Watch Series 5 has a cellular connectivity so that it can be used for phone calls, without the need to have an iPhone with you.

The Apple Watch Series 5 also has a host of useful apps, aimed at improving health and fitness: there is a new ECG app that includes an electrical heart sensor that can show your heart rhythm, a Noise app for measuring the sound level around you, and the Activity app for measuring daily exercise tasks. There is also a built-in fall detection function, and an International Emergency Calling option, to call the emergency services wherever you are in the world.

The Apple Watch Series 5 includes a Compass app, which, in conjunction with the Maps app, is ideal for displaying directions when you are out and about.

Wearable technology like the Apple Watch is growing rapidly, and there are likely to be more and more health and fitness features added as this technology evolves further.

Don't forget

The Apple Watch has to be "paired" with an iPhone, using the Watch app.

Hot tip

The App Store has a **Health & Fitness** category and also a **Medical** category, to cover a wide range of health-related issues. Many of the apps can be used with the Apple Watch.

Beware

If you have a pre-existing medical condition, or are on any medication, always consult your doctor before using a new health or fitness app that could have an impact on this.

Using the Health App

The Health app is available in iOS 13, and it enables you to input and analyze a wide range of health and fitness information. There are two main areas within the app:

Health

Summary

This displays an overview of items that have been specified to appear here. To use this:

1 Tap once on the **Summary** button on the bottom toolbar

Summary

2 The summary information is displayed for a range of health and fitness categories

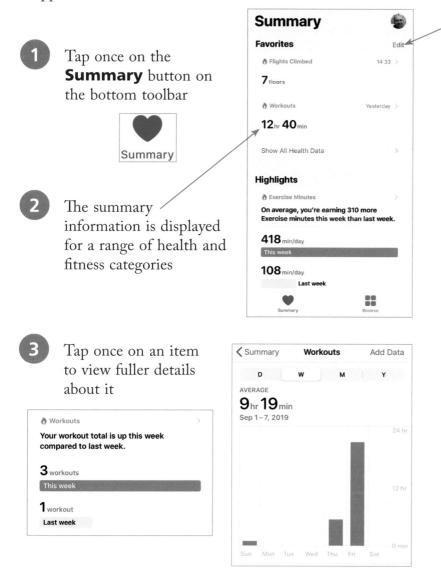

Summary

Favorites   Edit

🔥 Flights Climbed   14:33 >
7 floors

🔥 Workouts   Yesterday >
12 hr **40** min

Show All Health Data   >

Highlights

🔥 Exercise Minutes   >
On average, you're earning 310 more
Exercise minutes this week than last week.

418 min/day
This week

108 min/day
Last week

Summary   Browse

3 Tap once on an item to view fuller details about it

🔥 Workouts   >
Your workout total is up this week
compared to last week.

3 workouts
This week

1 workout
Last week

‹ Summary   **Workouts**   Add Data

D   **W**   M   Y

AVERAGE
9 hr **19** min
Sep 1–7, 2019

24 hr

12 hr

0 min
Sun   Mon   Tue   Wed   Thu   Fri   Sat

Hot tip

The items that appear on the Summary page can be edited, by tapping once on the **Edit** button in Step 1. On the Edit Favorites page, tap once next to the items that you want to appear, so that they have a solid star next to them.

Edit Favorites   Done

Existing Data   All

🔥 Activity

Active Energy   ★

Activity   ☆

Cycling Distance   ☆

Exercise Minutes   ★

Hot tip

Swipe up the Summary page to access the **Medical ID** section. This can be used to enter details in case of a medical emergency.

✳

Set Up Your Medical ID
In an emergency, first responders can look at your Medical ID to get life-saving information.

Get Started

...cont'd

The range of health and fitness categories has been updated in iOS 13.

Browse

This displays the available categories within the Health app, and shows any data that has been added for them.

 Tap once on the **Browse** button on the bottom toolbar

When adding data, do so at regular intervals, to build up a comprehensive set of results for analysis by the Health app.

2 The range of health and fitness categories is displayed. Swipe down the page to view more items

In addition to fitness categories, a range of medical information can also be entered and stored in the Health app, including specific medical conditions and immunizations.

3 Tap once on an item to view fuller details

4 For each item, health data can be entered manually (see next page)

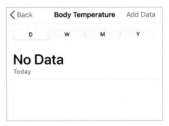

...cont'd

Adding health data
To enter data for the categories in the Health app:

 Tap once on the **Summary** button

2 Tap once on one of the categories on the Summary page

Workouts	Yesterday >
2 hr 40 min	

3 Tap once on the **Add Data** button **Add Data**

4 Enter the details for the selected item; e.g. entering the type and duration of a specific workout. Tap once on the **Add** button

Cancel	Workouts	Add
Activity Type		Tennis
Kilocalories		500
Distance (mi)		
Starts	Sep 7, 2020	14:00
Ends	Sep 7, 2020	16:00

5 The data is added for the selected item and this will be collated and stored within the Health app. Tap on these buttons to view the data for **Day**, **Week**, **Month**, and **Year**. Tap once on the **Summary** button to return to the main Summary page

< Summary

Health data can be added for the full range of categories in the **Browse** section by tapping once on the **Add Data** button in Step 4 on the previous page.

Some items in the Health app have data added automatically, such as Walking + Running, Steps, and Flights Climbed, in the Activity category.

See iPhone & Apple Watch for Health & Fitness in easy steps for more help on using these devices to achieve your health goals.

147

Jotting Down Notes

It is always useful to have a quick way of making notes of everyday things, such as shopping lists, recipes, or packing lists for traveling. On your iPhone, the Notes app is perfect for this function. To use it:

If iCloud is turned **On** for Notes (**Settings > Apple ID > iCloud > Notes**) then all of your notes will be stored here and will be available on any other iCloud-enabled devices that you have.

The first line of a note becomes its title when viewed in the list of all notes. (To view this, tap once on the **All iCloud** button).

 Tap once on the **Notes** app

 Tap once on this button on the bottom toolbar to create a new note

3 Enter text for the note

4 Tap once on this button to share (via Message or Mail, or any social media apps on your iPhone), copy or print a note

5 Tap once on this button to access the formatting toolbar. (Tap once on the cross to close the toolbar)

6 Double-tap on text to select it, and tap once on this button to access text formatting options

You can edit a note at any time by tapping on it once in the top-level folder and editing the text as required.

7 Tap once on this button to create a checklist. Add items to the list. Tap once on a check button to add a tick and show it as completed

For more information about selecting text, see page 91.

8 Tap once on this button to share the current note by Message, Mail, or a social media app and allow someone else to edit it

Press and hold firmly on the keyboard in Notes to activate it as a trackpad. You can then swipe over it to move the cursor around the screen.

9 Tap once on this button to add a handwritten item or drawing

10 Tap once on this button to add a photo or video to a note. Select a photo or video from your library, or take a new one

Scan Documents

Take Photo or Video

Photo Library

Cancel

Tap once on the **Scan Documents** button in Step 10 to scan a document into the current note.

11 The latest note appears at the top of the iCloud list. Each time a note is edited, it moves to the top. Swipe from right to left on a note and tap once on this button to delete it

All iCloud

Shopping
14:57   Stock cubes
🗀 Notes

Tap once on this icon on the bottom toolbar to delete the current note.

Keeping Up-to-Date

The Calendar app can be used to add events and appointments and keep yourself up-to-date with your daily, monthly, and annual activities.

1 Tap once on the **Calendar** app

2 If **Month** view is displayed, tap once here to access **Year** view. In Year view, tap once on a month to view it

3 Tap once on a day to view it (the current day is highlighted red)

4 Swipe up and down to view any events in **Day** view. Tap once on an event to view its details

Tap once on the **Today** button from any date to view the current date, in whichever view you are currently in.

Adding events

To add new events to the calendar:

1 Press and hold on a time slot within Day view, or tap once on this button

2 Enter a title for the event, and tap once on the **Starts** button to add a start time

3 Add an end time, by tapping on the **Ends** button, and also a repeat frequency (for recurring events such as birthdays). Select a specific calendar for the event and add an alert, if required. Tap once on the **Add** button to create the event

4 Tap once on this button to view a list of your current events and appointments

Hot tip

Drag the **All-day** button to **On** to set an event for the whole day, rather than adding specific start and end times.

Don't forget

The repeat frequency for an event can be set to every day, every week, every 2 weeks, every month, or every year. There is also a **Custom** option for specific time periods.

The Reminders app has been updated in iOS 13.

The items created under the **My Lists** heading are collated into the smart lists at the top of the window, according to items that have been added to them. For instance, if a reminder has had a flag added to it, it will appear in the **Reminders** list and also under the **Flagged** smart list. Any subsequent flagged lists will also appear here.

Setting Reminders

Another useful organization app is Reminders. This enables you to create lists for different topics and then set reminders for specific items. A date and time can be set for each reminder, and when this is reached the reminder appears on your iPhone screen. To use Reminders:

 Tap once on the **Reminders** app

 The items that have been created are listed under smart lists at the top of the window (collated according to the type of list) and also beneath the **My Lists** headings. This includes reminders and lists. Tap once on the **Edit** button to reorder or delete any of the My Lists items

3 Tap once on one of the smart lists to view the items that have been created within it

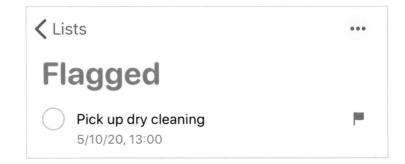

Creating reminders

To create new reminders and lists:

1 Tap once on one of the options; e.g. Reminders, and tap once on the **New Reminder** button

 New Reminder

2 Enter the title of the reminder and tap once on the **i** button to access the **Details** window

⟨ Lists   Done

Reminders

◯ Pick up dry cleaning   ⓘ

Don't forget

Once a reminder item has been created, it is displayed with any details next to it; e.g. time, location, flag or priority tag.

Reminders

◯ !! Pick up dry cleaning   🚩
  5/10/20, 13:00

3 Enter the details of the item, including a day and time for a reminder alert, a repeat schedule for the reminder, and a flag or priority tag for the reminder. Tap once on the **Done** button once the details for the reminder have been added

Details   Done

Pick up dry cleaning

Notes

URL

Remind me on a day   ⬤

Alarm   Sun, 5/10/20, 13:00

Remind me at a time   ⬤

Repeat   Never >

Remind me at a location   ◯

Remind me when messaging   ◯
Selecting this option will show the reminder notification when chatting with a person in Messages.

Flagged   ⬤

Priority   None >

4 When creating an entry for

the Reminders app, use the Quick Toolbar above the keyboard to, from left to right: add the time for the item; add a location for it; add a flag; or add a photo to the item

NEW

The Quick Toolbar is a new feature in iOS 13.

153

Recording Voice Memos

Voice memos are an increasingly popular way to send short voice messages to family and friends. They can also be used as a method of verbal note-taking when you want to remember something. To use voice memos:

1 Tap once on the **Voice Memos** app

2 Tap once on the red **Record** button to start recording a voice memo

3 Tap once on this button to finish recording

4 The memo is displayed in the main Voice Memos window. Tap once on the **Play** button to hear the recording

Voice Memos

Home
16:44   00:03

0:00   -0:03

•••   15   ▶   15   🗑

5 Tap once here and tap once on the **Edit Recording** button to amend the existing voice memo

Edit Recording

6 Tap once on this button in the top right-hand corner of the record window to trim the existing voice memo

7 Drag the yellow borders of a recording to trim its start and end points. Tap once on the **Trim** button to edit the recording

Trim

8 Tap once on the **Save** button to save the amended recording

Save

Hot tip

If the Voice Memos app is not readily visible, look in the **Utilities** folder on the second Home screen.

Don't forget

Tap once on the menu button, as accessed in Step 5, to **Duplicate** or **Share** a voice memo, in addition to editing a recording.

Getting the News

The iPhone with iOS 13 is ideal for keeping up with the news, whether you are on the move or at home. This is made even easier with the News app, which can be used to collate news stories from numerous online media outlets, covering hundreds of subjects. To use it:

1. Tap once on the **News** app

2. Tap once on the **Today** button on the bottom toolbar to view the latest stories in your news feed

3. The latest news stories are displayed, including specific categories such as Trending Stories

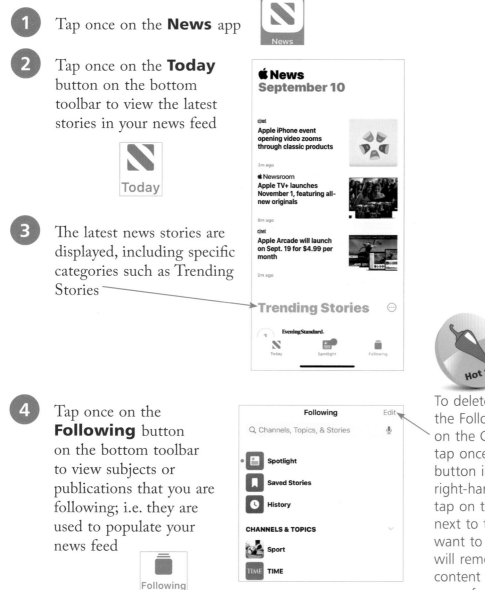

4. Tap once on the **Following** button on the bottom toolbar to view subjects or publications that you are following; i.e. they are used to populate your news feed

Hot tip

To delete an item from the Following section on the Channels page, tap once on the **Edit** button in the top right-hand corner, and tap on the red circle next to the item you want to delete. This will remove its related content from your news feed.

...cont'd

5 Under the **Suggested by Siri** heading, tap once on a **+** icon to include that subject or publication in your news feed

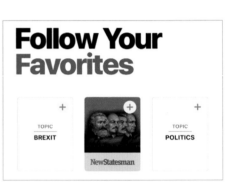

SUGGESTED BY SIRI

PoliticsHome   + ···

Tennis   ✓ ···

Tennis365   + ···

6 Scroll down the main Channels page and tap once on the **Discover Channels & Topics** button to add more subjects or publications

PERSONALIZE YOUR NEWS
Follow your favorite channels and topics to improve your reading experience.

Discover Channels & Topics

7 Tap once on an item to add it to your Favorites (so it will show up in your news feed) and tap once on the **Done** button at the bottom of the window

Follow Your Favorites

+   +   +

TOPIC   NewStatesman   TOPIC
BREXIT   POLITICS

Done

8 When an article has been opened for reading, tap on these buttons on the bottom toolbar to, from left to right: change the text size of the article being read; or share the item with other people, using email, messaging or social media

Hot tip

Tap once on the **Spotlight** button on the bottom toolbar to view in-depth articles on subjects selected by Apple News.

Spotlight

10 Relaxing with your iPhone

This chapter shows how to get the most out of your iPhone for playing music, reading, and also online shopping.

Around the iTunes Store

The iPhone performs an excellent role as a mobile entertainment center: its versatility means that you can carry your music, videos, and books in your pocket. Much of this content comes from the online iTunes Store. To access this and start adding content to your iPhone:

Although iTunes has been removed from Mac computers with the macOS operating system, the iTunes Store is still a part of iOS 13 and can be used to download a range of content, including music and movies. These items are then displayed in their respective apps; i.e. the Music and TV apps.

Don't forget

Tap once on the **Genres** button at the top of the Music Homepage to view items for different musical genres and styles.

Genres

Beware

Downloaded movies and TV shows take up a lot of storage space on the iPhone.

1 Tap once on the **iTunes Store** app

2 The iTunes Store interface is similar to the App Store. Tap once on the **Featured** or **Charts** tabs at the top of the window to view these headings

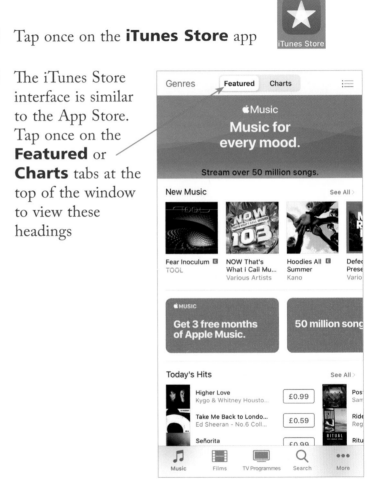

3 Use the buttons on the bottom toolbar to access content for Music, Films/Movies and TV Programmes/Shows

4 Swipe to the left and right on each panel to view items within it

Don't forget

Tap once on the **Charts** tab at the top of the iTunes Store window to view the top-ranking items for the category that is being viewed.

Charts

5 Swipe up and down to view more headings

6 Tap once on the **Films/Movies** button to view the movies in the iTunes Store. These can be bought or rented

7 Tap once on the **TV Programmes/Shows** button to view the TV shows in the iTunes Store. These can be bought or rented

Don't forget

To view all of your iTunes purchases, tap once on the **More** button on the bottom toolbar and tap once on the **Purchased** button. View your purchases by category (Music, Films/Movies or TV Programmes/ Shows), and tap once on the cloud symbol next to a purchased item to download it to your iPhone.

8 Tap once on the **More** button to access additional content

● ● ●

More

9 Tap once on the **Genius** button to view suggested content, based on what you have already bought from the iTunes Store

	More	Edit
🔔	Tones	>
⚛	Genius	>
♪	Purchased	>
⬇	Downloads	>

Buying Items

Once you have found the content you want in the iTunes Store, you can then buy it and download it to your iPhone.

Don't forget

If you have set up Apple Pay (see pages 54-55) you will be able to use this to buy items in the iTunes Store. Use the Face ID function – see page 24 – (or Touch ID for older iPhones with iOS 13) in Step 1, after you have tapped on the price button, to authorize the payment using Apple Pay.

1 For music items, tap once on the price button next to an item (either an album or individual songs) and follow the instructions. Tap once on the **Music** app to play the item (see next page)

Music

‹ Music			⬆
	Sunny Side Up		
	Paolo Nutini ›		
	Pop		
	14 Songs		£5.99
	Released May 29, 2009		
	★★★★☆ (1,081)		
Songs	Reviews		Related
1	**10 / 10**	02:56	£0.99
2	**Coming Up Easy**	04:18	£0.99
3	**Growing Up Beside You**	03:23	£0.99
4	**Candy**	04:58	£0.99
5	**Tricks of the Trade**	02:32	£0.99

Don't forget

For rented movies and TV shows, you have 30 days to watch an item after you have downloaded it. After you have started watching, you have 48 hours until it expires.

2 For movies and TV shows, tap once on the **Buy** or **Rent** button next to the title. Tap once on the **TV** app to play the item

TV

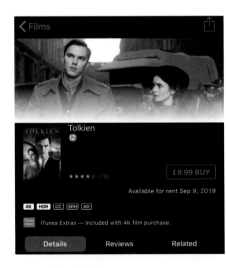

‹ Films

Tolkien
12

★★★★☆ (10)

£9.99 BUY

Available for rent Sep 9, 2019

4K HDR CC SDH AD

iTunes Extras — Included with 4K film purchase.

Details   Reviews   Related

Music on the iPhone

Once music has been bought from the iTunes Store, it can be played on your iPhone using the Music app. To do this:

 Tap once on the **Music** app

2 Tap once on the **Library** button on the bottom toolbar

3 Select one of the options for viewing items in the Library. This can be **Playlists**, **Artists**, **Albums**, **Songs**, and **Downloaded Music**

To create a playlist of songs, tap once on the **Playlists** button in Step 3, then tap once on the **New Playlist...** button. Give it a name and then add songs from your Library, using the **Add Music** button.

4 For the **Artists** section, tap once on an artist to view details of their songs on your iPhone

...cont'd

Tap once on this button in Step 5 to access a menu for the current track. This includes options to download the track, delete it from the Music app Library, add it to a playlist, or share it.

By default, music that has been bought from the iTunes Store is kept online and can be played on your iPhone by streaming it over Wi-Fi. However, it is also possible to download tracks to your iPhone so that you can play them without being online. Tap once on this button to download a specific track.

5 Select a track to play it

6 A limited version of the music controls appears at the bottom of the window

7 Tap once here to view the full version of the music controls. Use these buttons to return to the start of a track, play/pause a track, fast-forward, and adjust the volume

Using Apple Music

Apple Music is a service that makes the entire Apple iTunes Library of music available to users. It is a subscription service, but there is a three-month free trial. Music can be streamed over the internet or downloaded so you can listen to it when you are offline. To start with Apple Music:

1 Tap once on the **Music** app

2 Tap once on the **For You** button

3 Tap once on the **Choose Your Plan** button. (This option is available if you have already used the free, three-month trial of Apple Music)

4 Select the type of plan to which you want to subscribe, and tap once on the **Join Apple Music** button. Once you have joined Apple Music, you will be able to select the music genres in which you are most interested and receive suggestions based on this. You will also be able to listen to the entire iTunes Library of music

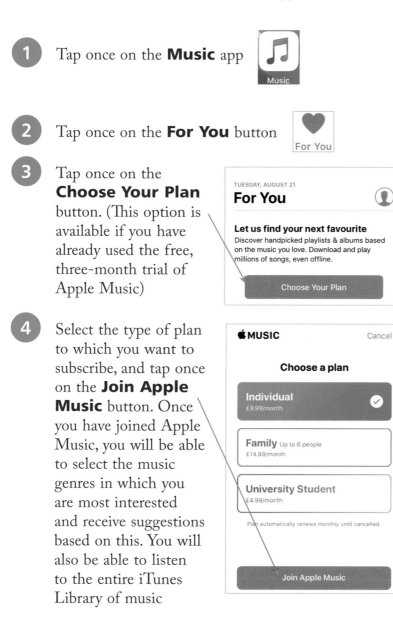

TUESDAY, AUGUST 21

For You

Let us find your next favourite
Discover handpicked playlists & albums based on the music you love. Download and play millions of songs, even offline.

Choose Your Plan

 MUSIC Cancel

Choose a plan

Individual
£9.99/month ✓

Family Up to 6 people
£14.99/month

University Student
£4.99/month

Plan automatically renews monthly until cancelled.

Join Apple Music

Hot tip

To end your Apple Music subscription at any point (and to ensure you do not subscribe at the end of the free trial), open the **Settings** app. Tap once on the **iTunes & App Store** button, and tap once on your own **Apple ID** link (in blue). Tap once on the **View Apple ID** button and enter your Apple ID password. Under **Subscriptions**, tap once on the **Manage** button. Drag the **Automatic Renewal** button **Off**. You can then renew your Apple Music membership, if required, by selecting one of the **Renewal Options**. If you do not renew your subscription once the free trial finishes, you will not be able to access any music that you have downloaded during the trial.

163

Reading

In addition to audio and visual content from the iTunes Store, it is also possible to read books on your iPhone using the Books app. To do this:

 Tap once on the **Books** app

 Tap once on the **Reading Now** button on the bottom toolbar to view any items you have in your Library

 If a title has a cloud icon next to it, tap once on this to download the book to your iPhone

---

Hot tip

Although not as large as a book or an electronic book reader, all of the iPhones are acceptable for reading books, particularly if you are traveling.

4 Tap once on the **Library** button on the bottom toolbar to view books that have been downloaded and added to the Library section

5 Tap once on a title to open it for reading. Tap once here to access options for browsing collections within the Library; e.g. looking for books in certain categories such as Crime and Romance

6 Tap once on the **Book Store** button on the bottom toolbar to view books in the Book Store

Hot tip

If you have a Kindle account, you can download the Kindle app from the App Store and use this to connect to your account and all of the books within it.

Kindle
Read eBooks & Magazines
★★★★★ 52.6K

Don't forget

Once books have been downloaded to your iPhone, tap once on a title in the **Library** section to read it. Tap on the left or right of the screen to move between pages, or swipe from the left or right edges. Tap in the middle of a page to activate the reading controls at the top of the screen, including Table of Contents, text size, and color options.

Shopping

Online shopping was one of the first great commercial successes on the web. Thousands of retailers now have their own websites and, increasingly, their own apps that can be used on the iPhone. So there are now more options than ever for online shopping:

Don't forget

For some online retailers, you will have to register and create an account before you can buy items. For others, you will be able to go straight to the checkout and enter your payment details.

Don't forget

A number of online retailers offer Apple Pay (see pages 54-55) as a method of payment, denoted by the Apple Pay logo. The number of retailers offering this is likely to grow considerably as Apple Pay becomes more widely available.

1 Download apps from the App Store for well-known retailers such as Amazon and eBay

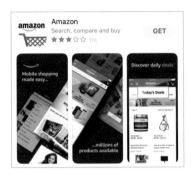

2 Use Safari and look up the retailer's website (in some cases, the website will have an option to download the app too)

3 Some websites will only enable you to download the retailer's app and use this

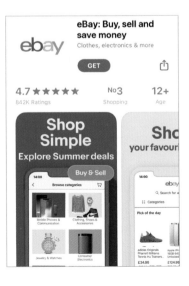

Comparing prices

Online retailing has also made it a lot easier to compare prices between sites. This can be done in two main ways:

1 Use Safari and search for price comparison websites. Different sites specialize in different products and services, so you may want to use a number of them

Hot tip

Another option for comparing prices is to check them in a bricks-and-mortar shop, and then compare them with the online prices.

2 There are apps in the App Store that can be used to scan barcodes of products and then compare prices for a specific item across different retailers

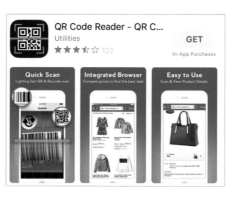

Researching

With your iPhone in your hand, you literally have a world of information at your fingertips. Whatever your hobby or interest, you will be able to find out a lot more about it using several different options:

1 Press and hold on the **On/Off** button (or the **Home** button for older iPhones) to access **Siri** and make an enquiry this way

2 Use the **App Store** to search for apps for your chosen subject

By default, the search engine used by Safari is Google. However, this can be changed in **Settings** > **Safari** > **Search Engine**.

3 Search **Safari** to find related websites and also general information about a specific topic

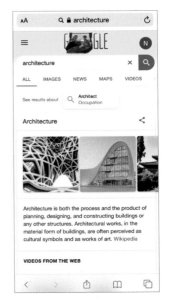

11 On the Go

The iPhone is a great companion whenever you are out and about anywhere, whether at home or abroad.

The Maps app works best if you have Location Services turned On, so that it can show your current location and give directions in relation to this. To turn on Location Services, go to **Settings** > **Privacy** > **Location Services** > **Maps** and tap once on **While Using the App**.

When you tap in the Maps Search box it expands towards the top of the screen. Below the Search box are options for adding favorite locations. Tap once on a location to add its details or tap once on the **Add** button to include a new location. This is a new feature in iOS 13.

Finding Locations

Finding locations around the world is only ever a couple of taps away when you have your iPhone and the Maps app.

1 Tap once on the **Maps** app

2 The Search box is at the bottom of the window

3 Enter an item into the Search box. As you type, suggestions appear underneath. Tap on one to go to that location

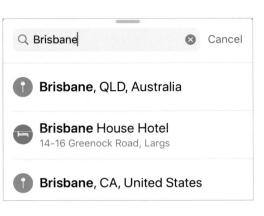

4 For the current location, options for searching over items such as food outlets, shops, and entertainment are available.

Tap on one of these to see results for these categories in the current location

5 The location selected in Step 3 is displayed, with information about it at the bottom of the window

Don't forget

Some locations, such as airports and shopping centers, can display indoor layouts.

6 Swipe up from the bottom of the window to view full details about the location, including photos, address, phone number, and website address, if available

Hot tip

Some locations have a 3D Flyover Tour feature. This is an automated tour of a location, featuring its most notable sites. It covers major cities around the world, and the list is regularly being added to. If it is available for a location, tap once on the **Flyover** button at the bottom of the window, next to the **Directions** button. Tap once on the **Start City Tour** button to start the Flyover Tour. Try it with a location such as New York, London or Paris.

7 At the top of the Maps app window, tap once on this icon for map style options

8 Select either **Standard (Map)**, **Transit** or **Satellite** to view the map in that style

171

Getting Directions

Wherever you are in the world, you can get directions between two locations. To do this:

Hot tip

You can enter the Start point as your current location. Tap once on this button to view your current location.

Beware

If you enter the name of a landmark you may also be shown other items that have the same name, such as businesses.

Hot tip

For some destinations, alternative routes will be displayed, depending on distance and traffic conditions. Tap once on the alternative route to select it. Directions for each route can be selected at the bottom of the window.

1 Tap once in the Search box at the bottom of the window in the Maps app

2 Enter the destination (by default, this is from your current location)

3 Tap once on the **Directions** button. The route is shown on the map

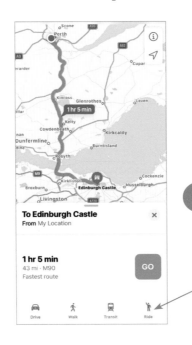

4 Tap once on these buttons at the bottom of the window to view the route for **Drive**, **Walk**, **Transit**, or a taxi **Ride** using an appropriate app

5 Tap once on the **Go** button to view step-by-step instructions on the map

6 The route is displayed, from your starting location. Audio instructions tell you the directions to be followed. You can use the Volume buttons (on the side of the iPhone) to increase or decrease the sound. As you follow the route, the map and instructions are updated

The arrow in Step 6 points in the current direction of travel; i.e. the direction in which the iPhone is pointing.

173

7 Swipe up from the bottom of the screen to access options for viewing items such as gas stations and food outlets on the route. These are displayed on the map, in relation to the current route being followed

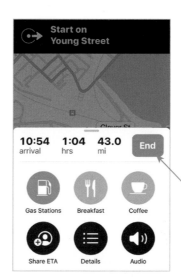

Tap once on the **End** button and then the **End Route** button to stop following the current route.

Booking a Trip

Most major travel retailers have had their own websites for a number of years. They have now moved into the world of apps, and these can be used on your iPhone to book almost any type of vacation, from cruises to city breaks.

Several apps for the iPhone (and their associated websites) offer full travel services where they can deal with flights, hotels, insurance, car hire, and excursions. These include:

- **Expedia**
- **Kayak**
- **Orbitz**
- **Travelocity**

These apps usually list special offers and last-minute deals on their Homepages, and they offer options for booking flights, hotels, car hire, and activities separately.

Hot tip

It is always worth searching different apps to get the best possible price. In some cases, it is cheapest to buy different elements of a vacation from different retailers; e.g. flights from one seller and accommodation from another.

Don't forget

Most travel apps have specific versions based on your geographical location. You will be directed to these by default.

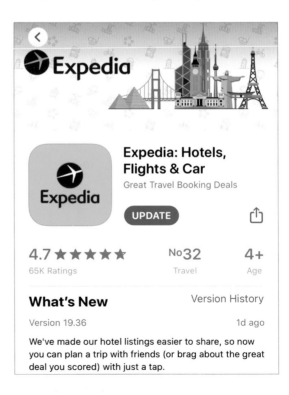

Expedia

Expedia: Hotels, Flights & Car
Great Travel Booking Deals

Expedia

UPDATE

4.7 ★★★★★
65K Ratings

No32
Travel

4+
Age

What's New   Version History

Version 19.36   1d ago

We've made our hotel listings easier to share, so now you can plan a trip with friends (or brag about the great deal you scored) with just a tap.

TripAdvisor

One of the best resources for travelers is TripAdvisor. Not only does the app provide a full range of opportunities for booking flights and hotels, it also has an extensive network of reviews from people who have visited the countries, hotels, and restaurants on the site. These are independent, and usually very fair and honest. In a lot of cases, if there are issues with a hotel or restaurant, the proprietor posts a reply to explain what is being done to address any problems.

Don't forget

TripAdvisor has a certain sense of community, so post your own reviews once you have been places, to let others know about your experience.

175

Cruises

There are also apps dedicated specifically to cruises. One to look at is iCruise, which searches over a range of companies for your perfect cruise vacation.

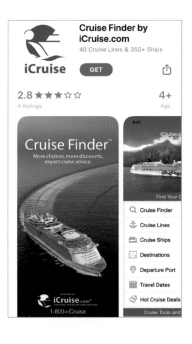

Booking Hotels

The internet is a perfect vehicle for finding good-value hotel rooms around the world. When hotels have spare capacity, this can quickly be relayed to associated websites and apps, where users can often benefit from cheap prices and special offers. There are plenty of apps that have details of thousands of hotels around the world, such as:

Trivago
An app that searches over one million hotels on more than 250 sites, to ensure you get the right hotel for the best price.

Hotels.com
A stylish app that enables you to enter search keywords into a Search box on the Home screen to find hotels based on destination, name, or local landmarks.

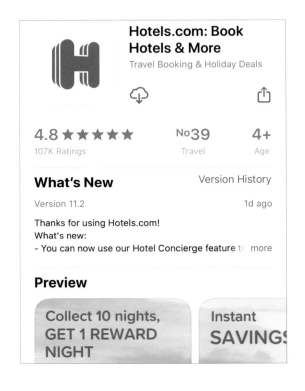

Hotels.com: Book Hotels & More

Travel Booking & Holiday Deals

4.8 ★★★★★   No39   4+
107K Ratings   Travel   Age

What's New   Version History

Version 11.2   1d ago

Thanks for using Hotels.com!
What's new:
- You can now use our Hotel Concierge feature t more

Preview

Collect 10 nights, GET 1 REWARD NIGHT

Instant SAVINGS

Booking.com
Another good, fully-featured hotel app that provides a comprehensive service and excellent prices.

LateRooms.com
An app that specializes in getting the best prices by dealing with rooms that are available at short notice. Some genuine bargains can be found here, for hotels of all categories.

Hot tip

Most hotel apps have reviews of all of the listed establishments. It is always worth reading these, as it gives you a view from the people who have actually been there.

Hot tip

Currency converters can also be downloaded from the App Store so that you can see how much your money is worth in different countries.

Finding Flights

Flying is a common part of modern life and although you do not have to book separate flights for a vacation (if it is part of a package), there are a number of apps for booking flights and also for following the progress of those in the air:

Skyscanner Travel Deals

This app can be used to find flights at airports around the world. Enter your details such as leaving airport, destination and dates of travel. The results show a range of available options, covering different price ranges and airlines.

Flight apps need to have an internet connection in order to show real-time flight information.

177

Flightradar24

If you like viewing the path of flights that are in the air, or need to check if flights are going to be delayed, this app provides this inflight information. Flights are shown according to flight number and airline.

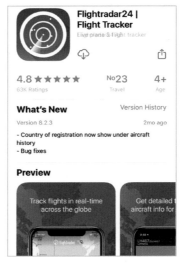

FlightAware Flight Tracker

Another app for tracking flights, showing arrivals and departures and also information about delays. It can track commercial flights worldwide.

Speaking their Language

When you are traveling abroad, it is always beneficial to learn some of the language of the country you are visiting. With your iPhone at hand this has become a whole lot easier, and there are a number of options:

1 Translation apps that can be used to translate words, phrases and sentences in every language you probably need

Some language apps are free, but they then charge for additional content, known as "in-app purchases".

2 Language apps that offer options in several languages

3 Specific language apps, where you can fully get to grips with a new language

12 Practical Matters

This chapter looks at accessibility and security.

Accessibility Issues

The iPhone tries to cater to as wide a range of users as possible, including those who have difficulty with visual, hearing, or physical and motor issues. There are a number of settings that can help with these areas. To access the range of Accessibility settings:

Don't forget

You will have to scroll down the page to view the full range of Accessibility options.

Hot tip

Tap once on **Vision** > **Display & Text Size** and drag the **On/Off Labels** button **On** to show the relevant icons on the On/Off buttons.

 Tap once on the **Settings** app

 Tap once on the **Accessibility** tab

3 The settings for **Vision**, **Physical and Motor**, **Hearing**, and **General** are displayed here

⟨ Settings	**Accessibility**

Accessibility features help you customize your iPhone for your individual needs.

VISION

🔊 VoiceOver	Off >
⊙ Zoom	Off >
🔍 Magnifier	Off >
AA Display & Text Size	>
◎ Motion	>
💬 Spoken Content	>
💬 Audio Descriptions	Off >

PHYSICAL AND MOTOR

👆 Touch	>
😐 Face ID & Attention	>
⊞ Switch Control	Off >
😊 Voice Control	Off >

⟨ Settings	**Accessibility**

👆 Touch	>
😐 Face ID & Attention	>
⊞ Switch Control	Off >
😊 Voice Control	Off >
🔘 Side Button	>
📱 Apple TV Remote	>
⌨ Keyboards	>

HEARING

👂 Hearing Devices	>
🔊 Audio/Visual	>
💬 Subtitles & Captioning	>

GENERAL

🔒 Guided Access	Off >
✦ Siri	>
🧍 Accessibility Shortcut	Off >

...cont'd

Vision settings

These can help anyone with impaired vision. There are options to hear items on the screen and also for making text easier to read:

1 Tap once on the **VoiceOver** link

> 🔊 VoiceOver   Off ›

2 Drag this button **On** to activate the VoiceOver function. This then enables items to be spoken when you tap on them

3 Select options for VoiceOver as required, such as speaking rate and pitch

4 Tap once on an item to select it (indicated by the black outline) and have it read out. Double-tap to activate a selected item or perform an action

> ‹ Accessibility **VoiceOver**
>
> VoiceOver   ⬤
>
> VoiceOver speaks items on the screen:
> · Tap once to select an item
> · Double-tap to activate the selected item
> · Swipe three fingers to scroll

VoiceOver works with the built-in iPhone apps and some apps from the App Store, but not all of them.

Another useful Accessibility function is **AssistiveTouch**, within the **Physical and Motor** > **Touch** section. This offers a range of options for accessing items via tapping on the screen, rather than having to use swiping with two or more fingers. Tap once on this icon to access the items within AssistiveTouch after it has been turned **On**.

...cont'd

Zoom settings

Although the iPhone screens are among the largest in the smartphone market, there are times when it can be beneficial to increase the size of the items that are being viewed. This can be done with the Zoom feature. To use this:

1 Access the

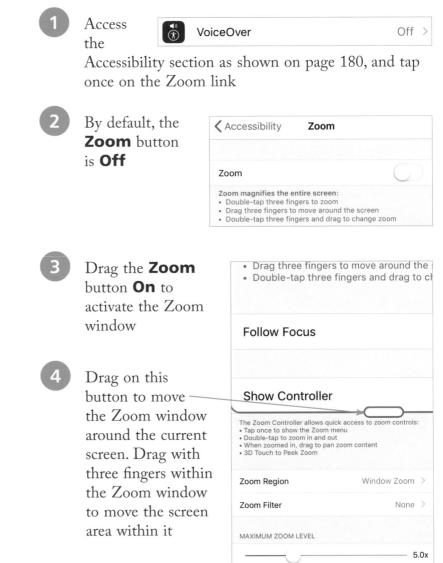

| VoiceOver | Off > |

Accessibility section as shown on page 180, and tap once on the Zoom link

2 By default, the **Zoom** button is **Off**

〈 Accessibility   **Zoom**

Zoom

Zoom magnifies the entire screen:
- Double-tap three fingers to zoom
- Drag three fingers to move around the screen
- Double-tap three fingers and drag to change zoom

3 Drag the **Zoom** button **On** to activate the Zoom window

- Drag three fingers to move around the
- Double-tap three fingers and drag to ch

Follow Focus

Show Controller

4 Drag on this button to move the Zoom window around the current screen. Drag with three fingers within the Zoom window to move the screen area within it

The Zoom Controller allows quick access to zoom controls:
- Tap once to show the Zoom menu
- Double-tap to zoom in and out
- When zoomed in, drag to pan zoom content
- 3D Touch to Peek Zoom

| Zoom Region | Window Zoom > |
| Zoom Filter | None > |

MAXIMUM ZOOM LEVEL

5.0x

Hot tip

Drag the **Show Controller** button **On** in the Zoom settings to display a control button for the Zoom window. Tap once on the control button to view its menu of additional features, such as zooming in to greater or lesser amounts.

5 The Zoom window can also be used on the keyboard to increase the size of the keys. As in Step 4, drag with three fingers to move to other parts of the keyboard

Text size can also be increased within the Accessibility settings. To do this:

1 Under the **Vision** section, tap once on the **Display & Text Size** link

AA Display & Text Size >

2 Tap once on the **Larger Text** button   Larger Text

3 Drag the **Larger Accessibility Sizes** button **On** to enable compatible apps to show larger text sizes

4 Drag this slider to set the text size

Finding your iPhone

No-one likes to think the worst, but if your iPhone is lost or stolen, help is at hand. The Find My iPhone function (operated through the iCloud service) allows you to locate a lost iPhone, and send a message and an alert to it. You can also remotely lock it, or even wipe its contents. This gives added peace of mind, knowing that even if your iPhone is lost or stolen, its contents will not necessarily be compromised. To set up Find My iPhone:

Hot tip

Location Services has to be turned **On** to enable the Find My iPhone service. This can be done in the Settings app (**Settings** > **Privacy** > **Location Services** and drag the **Location Services** button **On**).

Hot tip

If you are using Family Sharing (see pages 64-67), you can use the Find My app to locate the devices of other Family Sharing members. This can be done from your online iCloud account, or with the Find My app.

1 Tap once on the **Settings** app and tap once on the Apple Account ID button

2 Tap once on the **Find My** button

3 Tap once on the **Find My iPhone** link (if it is showing **Off**. If it is **On** then Find My iPhone is already activated)

4 Drag the **Find My iPhone** button **On** to be able to find your iPhone on a map

Finding a lost iPhone

Once you have set up Find My iPhone, you can search for it through the iCloud service. To do this:

 Log in to your iCloud account at **www.icloud.com** and tap once on the **Find iPhone** button (you also have to sign in again with your Apple ID)

2   Tap once on the **All Devices** button and select your iPhone. It is identified, and its current location is displayed on the map

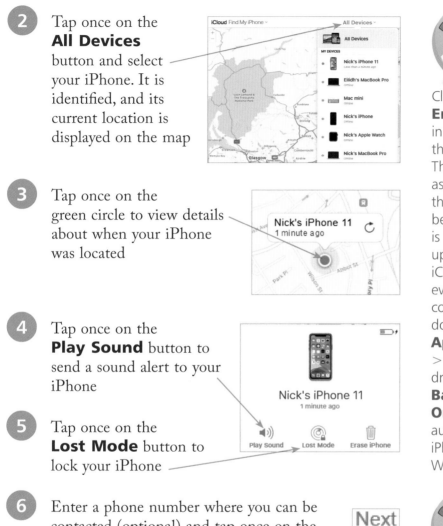

3   Tap once on the green circle to view details about when your iPhone was located

4   Tap once on the **Play Sound** button to send a sound alert to your iPhone

5   Tap once on the **Lost Mode** button to lock your iPhone

6   Enter a phone number where you can be contacted (optional) and tap once on the **Next** button

7   A message can also be added to be displayed on the lost iPhone. Tap once on the **Done** button to lock the iPhone. It is locked using its existing passcode, which is required to unlock it

Don't forget

Click once on the **Erase iPhone** button in Step 4 to delete the iPhone's contents. This should be done as a last resort if you think the contents may be compromised. It is important to back up your iPhone to iCloud in case you do ever have to erase its contents. This can be done in **Settings > Apple ID > iCloud > iCloud Backup** by dragging the **iCloud Backup** button to **On**. Backups are done automatically when the iPhone is connected to Wi-Fi (see page 61).

185

Don't forget

If you have Apple Pay set up on your iPhone, this will be suspended if Lost Mode is enabled. It will be reactivated when the passcode is entered to unlock it and your Apple ID entered within Settings.

Avoiding Viruses

As far as security from viruses on the iPhone is concerned, there is good news and bad news:

- The good news is that, due to its architecture, most apps on the iPhone do not communicate with each other unless specifically required to, such as the Mail and the Contacts apps. So, even if there were a virus, it would be difficult for it to infect the whole iPhone. Also, Apple performs rigorous tests on apps that are submitted to the App Store (although even this is not foolproof; see next bullet point).

- The bad news is that no computer system is immune from viruses and malware, and complacency is one of the biggest enemies of computer security. The iPhone's popularity means it is an attractive target for hackers and virus writers. There have been instances of photos in iCloud being accessed and hacked, but this was more to do with password security, or lack of, than viruses. There have also been some rare, malicious attacks centered around the code used to create apps for the App Store. In some cases, certain apps were affected before the virus was located and remedial action taken. This is a reminder of the need for extreme vigilance against viruses, and for users to check in the media for information about any new attacks. Search the web for "latest viruses" to find websites that specialize in identifying the latest software viruses and threats.

Antivirus options

There are a few apps in the App Store that deal with antivirus issues, although not actually removing viruses. Two options to look at are:

- **McAfee** apps. The online security firm has a number of apps that cover issues such as privacy and passwords.

- **Norton** apps. Similar to McAfee, Norton offers a range of security apps for the iPhone.

Malware is short for malicious software, designed to harm your iPhone or access and distribute information from it.

Apple also checks apps that are provided through the App Store, and this process is very robust. This does not mean that it is impossible for a virus to infect the iPhone, so keep an eye on the Apple website to see if there are any details about iPhone viruses.

G

H

I

K